"Every ethnic minority in seeking its
own freedom, helped strengthen
the fabric of liberty in American life."
—John F. Kennedy
from *A Nation of Immigrants*

MINORITIES ALL
chronicles the backbreaking and heartbreaking
stories of America's many ethnic groups as they
struggled against poverty, fear, and intolerance
to take their place in American society.

PROBLEMS OF AMERICAN SOCIETY

Focusing on the urban scene, youth, the individual and his search for a better life, the books in this series probe the most crucial dilemmas of our time.

* Forthcoming

GERALD
LEINWAND

MINORITIES
ALL

WSP
WASHINGTON SQUARE PRESS · NEW YORK

MINORITIES ALL

Washington Square Press edition published March, 1971

L

Published by
Washington Square Press, a division of Simon & Schuster, Inc.,
630 Fifth Avenue, New York, N.Y.

WASHINGTON SQUARE PRESS editions are distributed in the
U.S. by Simon & Schuster, Inc., 630 Fifth Avenue, New
York, N.Y. 10020 and in Canada by Simon & Schuster
of Canada, Ltd., Richmond Hill, Ontario, Canada.

1 2 3 4 5 2 1

ACKNOWLEDGMENT

This is one of a series of volumes designed to become text materials for urban schools. For their participation in making this possible the authors wish to thank the authors and publishers who permitted their articles to be reproduced here. We are in debt also to the many with whom selected portions of the manuscript were discussed. The cooperation of the editorial staff of Washington Square Press was indispensable to the successful completion of the volume. We are deeply grateful.

The people of the city are many. . . .
(New York Times photos)

Preface

The people of the city are many. They come from diverse racial, ethnic, religious, and geographic backgrounds. They have had vastly differing experiences and see themselves and their surroundings in very different ways. Because of these differences it is difficult to describe the characteristics which the people of the city have in common. As members of the human community, they are motivated, in varying degrees, to lead the good life in the city and to secure this good life for their children. What the people of the city also have in common is that nearly all of them are newcomers.

It was Oscar Handlin who applied the term "newcomers" to the most recent migrants, the blacks and the Puerto Ricans who in many ways play the role today that the immigrant played yesterday. But in a real sense, we are all newcomers; it does not take much digging into one's past to find that a parent, grandparent, or perhaps even a great grandparent, came to the city as a deliberate act of his rational will. He made up his mind to leave the land where he was born, to come to America, to settle in and build its cities. He did so knowing the hardships that would await him and the problems he would have in adjusting to a new way of life. Those experiences, adjustments, and struggles have influenced his descendants in a thousand ways.

Preface

One often speaks about "rugged individualism" as a characteristic of Americans. One implication of this statement is that each American makes up his own mind on the issues of the day. Recent evidence suggests, however, that few of us make up our minds uninfluenced by others. That influence comes most often from the group of which we are a part. When the ideas of one group differ from those of another, conflict may result. One writer has suggested that group conflict is "as American as cherry pie." Americans are either immigrants or the children of immigrants. Racially, the population includes not only Caucasians (whites) but blacks, Mexican-Americans, Indians, Chinese, Japanese, and Puerto Ricans. Most Americans are Protestants (in 222 denominations and sects). There are about 50 million Roman Catholics and 5.5 million Jews. The U.S.A., therefore, can be seen as a nation of groups as well as a nation of individuals. Any city is made up of a host of racial, religious, and ethnic groups striving for similar but not identical ends.

Conflict is inevitable but conflict can be beneficial. As each group is absorbed into city life, it becomes an example which groups not yet absorbed can hope to follow. This book is an attempt to show the common origins of the people of the city and the differences their experiences have created. As do other books in this series, it tries to raise questions rather than find answers. It tries to provide an elementary introduction to the problems and the prospects of the city's people. The people *are* the city and what happens to them determines the fate of the city in history.

G. L.

Contents

Contents

Part One

The Problem and the Challenge

(Joe Molnar)

I N the Upper West Side of New York City, an area
west of Fifth Avenue from 59th Street to 125th
Street, live more than 300,000 people of different
races, creeds, and cultures. About 100,000 Hispanic
Americans (Puerto Ricans, Dominicans, Cubans,
Mexicans) and about 60,000 Negroes live here,
together with Jews, Irish Catholics, and Anglo-Saxon
Protestants, as well as some Asiatics (Chinese,
Japanese, and Koreans).

The small businesses of the West Side reflect the
mixed nature of the area. Kosher butcher shops are
frequented by Puerto Ricans as well as Jews. The
owner of "La Gran Esquina Barbershop" makes
sure that his customers know that he is their "Barber
and Friend from Santo Domingo." There are many
Chinese restaurants, several Israeli night spots selling the *felafel*, an Israeli snack, and McGlade's,
an old-fashioned Irish tavern. Refugees from
Hitler's Germany live next door to American-born
and foreign-born Japanese. Churches and synagogues are plentiful and serve worshippers of all
religions and creeds, including the 800 who prefer
to worship at the New York Buddhist Church. The
West Side is unique because in its boundaries live
a generous sampling of the city's people. The more
one understands them, the more one understands
and appreciates the city itself.[1]

How Did the City Change the American Character?

The census of 1920 marked the end of America as a rural nation. Until that time most of the people of the United States lived in the country. But sometime between 1910, when the last census was taken, and 1920, when the new one was completed, the majority of the population became city-dwellers. An examination of the people of any city of 50,000 or more would find that most of these people were newcomers, either immigrants or recent descendants of immigrants. In general, the larger the city the greater the percentage of the total population who were foreign-born.

Once the nature of the population changed from mainly rural to mainly urban, the quality and character of the nation changed as well. The rural population which, up to 1920, made up the majority of the people, was mainly white and Protestant. Mostly they had come from countries of northern Europe, including the United Kingdom, Scandinavia, France, and Germany. In the rural communities in which they lived, people were more socially alike than different. Class differences existed, but in general, among rural, white Protestants these differences were not sharp. The well-to-do and the less prosperous valued hard work, self-help, self-discipline, and thrift.[2]

Even during colonial days life was different in the cities of America. The population was more varied. There were Catholics as well as Jews, people with strange accents, and people with black skin. Class differences were sharp and foreign newcomers could be seen everywhere. Americans usually think that the farm and the small town represented that which was worthwhile in American life. This was the Jeffersonian ideal of a country of independent farmers, skilled craftsmen and small-town people. The city was regarded as the den of political corruption and of all forms of wickedness and violence. People worked in shops and factories, joined labor unions, and struck for higher wages and shorter hours. Some held dangerous ideas—ideas they brought with them from strange lands.

The late President Franklin D. Roosevelt reminded the Daughters of the American Revolution that America was made up of both immigrants and revolutionists and that the Society had better not forget it. The city too was made up of immigrants from abroad and newcomers from rural America itself. They brought with them and continue to bring with them revolutionary ideas which are shaping the cities anew. They are reshaping the life and destiny of America as well.

Why and How Did Immigrants Come to the City?

If any one description fits America it may well be the late President John F. Kennedy's: "A Nation of Immigrants." About 150,000 immigrants came during the decade of the 1820's, and 1.7 million came twenty years later. In 1870, 2.8 million came and 5.2 million in the 1880's. The years between 1900 and 1910 saw the crest of immigration when 8.8 million immigrants arrived. After that date, immigration to America declined as laws limiting the number of immigrants that could be admitted in any one year went into effect. The decline continued until recent years when legislation urged by President Kennedy permitted a very modest rise.

The newcomers to the city before 1920 were mostly immigrants. An immigrant may be defined as anyone who moves from the country of his birth to live permanently in another. The only American, it has often been stated, is the Indian. But thousands of years ago even the Indian himself may have been an immigrant. Having endured generations of hardship, he may have hiked his way across the Bering Strait to Alaska to make his home in what centuries later came to be called the Americas. While there are other theories of how the first settlers came to North and South America, the important thing to keep in mind is that in a real sense no one is native to America. Even the earliest inhabitants who may be found here came from someplace else.

The reasons immigrants came to America were many but may perhaps be summarized simply under a few headings. Some came to seek religious or political freedom or to escape religious or political persecution. Others came because they thought the streets of America were "paved with gold" and they could make a better living for themselves and their families. Some were lured to America through the power of advertising as the steamship companies and the newly built railroads of America sought passengers. Blacks from Africa came because slave traders forced them to come.

The decision to leave their homeland, to uproot themselves from a life they knew, and to attempt to plant roots in a country whose life was unknown was but the beginning of a journey of incredible difficulty. The cost of passage took all or nearly all their savings. Some had to work their way from the village where they lived to the port from which their ship was to leave. Many had to wait in port in cheap, sordid and overcrowded boarding houses until a ship was available to take them. Here they sometimes lost their money to cutthroats or ex-

It is true that most of the early immigrants were the poor of their land, enticed by steamship ads telling of land and employment with good wages across the ocean. But if they were truly "wretched" and "tempest tossed" as the inscription on the Statue of Liberty suggests, it was probably due to the conditions they suffered on the steamship as they crossed the ocean. (Museum of the City of New York)

hausted it, and themselves, while waiting. When the great day came to board the ship, leave-taking was painful and sorrowful. Parents left children and husbands left wives, promising to send for the rest of the family when enough money had been made in America and a place to live had been found.

In the 1840's and 1850's, the average trip from Liverpool, England, to New York took forty days. Some took much longer as the ship was at the mercy of the sea, the currents, and the winds. Later on, the wide use of the steamship cut down the amount of time that was needed to cross the ocean. For most immigrants the journey was one of filthy quarters, tasteless and inadequate food, and overwhelming fear of the sea. The late President

Kennedy described the passage they endured as follows:

> "For the immigrants, their shipboard world was the steerage, that confined space below deck, usually about seventy-five feet long and twenty-five feet wide. In many vessels no one over five and a half feet tall could stand upright. Here they lived their days and nights receiving their daily ration of vinegar-flavored water and trying to eke out sustenance from whatever provisions they had brought along. When their food ran out, they were often at the mercy of extortionate captains.
>
> "They huddled in their hard, cramped bunks, freezing when the hatches were open, stifling when they were closed. The only light came from a dim, swaying lantern. Night and day were indistinguishable. But they were ever aware of the treacherous winds and waves, the scampering of rats and the splash of burials. Disease—cholera, yellow fever, smallpox and dysentery—took their toll. One in ten failed to survive the crossing."[3]

If the passage of the white immigrant from Europe was full of torment, that of the black immigrant from Africa was far worse. The forced migration of blacks began in the 16th century when 900,000 men, women, and children were captured by other Africans and sold to Arabs, who then resold them to slave traders of Europe and America. During the 17th century, the number increased to 2,750,000 and to 7 million in the 18th century. During the 1800's, the number fell to 4 million as the Constitutional provision forbade the importation of slaves to America after 1807. Not all of these numbers came to the United States. Many went to South America and to the West Indies as well. But of all it may be said:

> "The slaves were driven on board cargo ships by whipping and caning, and were branded by a hot iron which caused painful swelling in their cheeks, arms or flanks. Many thought they were going to be eaten by white men, and in their terror stabbed, hanged, or drowned themselves."[4]

Immigrants came from Asia, too, mainly from China and Japan. The Chinese came during the 1840's and 1850's in the great China clippers and were dumped in the cities of the West Coast, notably San Francisco. Because they would work for lower wages, there was fear that they would take jobs away from Americans. As a result, Congress passed the Chinese Exclusion Act in 1882. It closed America to Chinese immigrants. The Japanese began to come in larger numbers after 1900, but their period of migration was relatively short. In 1907, through what was known as the Gentlemen's Agreement, Japan agreed to limit the number of Japanese who would be permitted to leave that country for America. The Chinese and Japanese lived in a hostile America. The change from being viewed as the "yellow peril" to that of equal citizenship with other Americans was a long and hard one. It has not yet been entirely won.

Why Did Immigrants Settle in Cities?

Between 1865 and 1910, immigrants made up between 13 and 15 percent of the total population of America. The bulk of these people lived east of the Mississippi and north of the Ohio River. New

New York's Lower East Side has always been inhabited by
new immigrants to the city because the rents are cheaper.
(The Jacob A. Riis Collection, Museum of the City of New
York)

Today it is a mixture of older immigrants not wanting to leave what has been their home since they arrived in this country, and newer migrants, mostly blacks, Puerto Ricans, and teenagers coming down from the suburbs seeking a more challenging existence.

(Nathan Farb)

(Anthony Mazzariello)

York, Massachusetts, Pennsylvania, and Illinois contained nearly half of the total immigrant population. Few newcomers to America could be found in the Southern states. While some immigrants, such as the Czechs, did move out into rural areas to become farmers, most immigrants settled in cities. Immigrants from Ireland, Russia, Italy, and Hungary were especially drawn to the city.

What made city-dwellers of the newcomers to America? There were many factors at work. Immigrants of one national group preferred to live among one another. By living together adjustments to American life became more gradual and therefore easier. They could help one another find jobs and in time of sickness and death they could comfort one another. Ties of common origin, blood relationships, and common language and heritage kept immigrants together in the great ethnic ghettoes of the city. Most immigrants, it must be remembered, came from small urban communities and it was the city and not the country that was more familiar to them. Most immigrants, moreover, lacked the skills required for farming; they also lacked the capital needed to buy farm machinery or the savings needed until they could harvest and sell their first crop. Even those who had come from the farms of Europe or Asia were slow to settle on the farms of America. After all, it was from the farm that they were, in a sense, escaping. Opportunity, so they thought, was for them to be found in the city.

While it is true that some immigrants were attracted to America by the hope of getting free land, most were attracted by the possibility of getting good jobs. The period that followed the Civil War to the outbreak of World War I was a period in which the American nation began to develop its

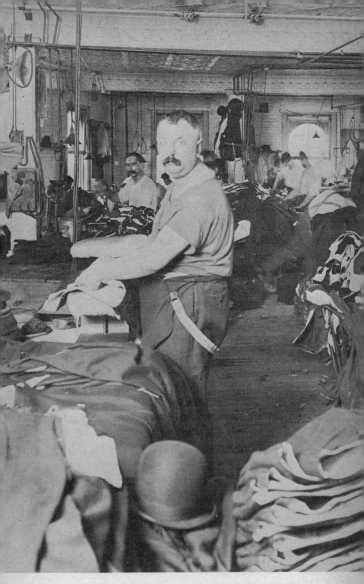

In 1921 the factories of the cities provided employment for most immigrants. (The Byron Collection, Museum of the City of New York)

industrial capacity at a very rapid rate. It needed
strong men to build the railroads, mine the coal,
operate the forges, slaughter the cattle, work the
machines, build the factories, pave the roads, dig
the tunnels, lay the tracks for the streetcars, and
string the wires for the telephones. It needed women,
too, to weave fabrics and operate the sewing machines and thus join the men in making the textile
industry possible. Unlike farming, most industry
required masses of unskilled labor and it was mainly
this need that immigrants filled.

In many ways, it is not quite accurate to say that
the immigrants "chose" to live in the city. In truth
they had no other choice. Driven to America by a
desire to escape undesirable conditions, they were
literally dumped in the ports of the New World.
And it was there that they remained, lacking as
they did the money to go further or the margin of
savings needed to support themselves while they
sought better living conditions.

Some attempts were made to settle the immigrants
inland. It was hoped that in this way the "burden"
of the newcomer would be more equitably distributed. The hostility to the newcomer would diminish
as his presence became less visible. Various Jewish
groups tried to build rural communities in the West
and South between 1881 and 1883. Sicily Island,
Louisiana; New Odessa, Oregon; and Catopoxi,
Colorado were among these.[5] The Irish Catholic
Colonization Association likewise sought to spread
the Irish, the most urban of the immigrant groups,
in the rural West. The efforts to get Jews and Irish
out of the city and onto the farm failed. While
many of both groups found their way from the cities
of the East coast to those of the mid- and far West,

it was in the city that they finally established themselves. Their destiny was tied to the city.

Before World War II the United States reluctantly opened its doors to the immigrant once again, this time to those who were seeking safety from the brutality of the Third Reich and Nazi Germany. Seventy percent of these immigrants were Jews and almost 40 percent of the newcomers were business and professional people. Some did not have a great deal of trouble finding employment with the skills and the capital that they brought with them and some were able to start new businesses of their own. But most, stripped of their resources, separated from families, crushed by Nazi brutality, scarred by the concentration camp, found as much difficulty as any other immigrant group in finding a place in American life. With tattooed numbers burned in their arms and souls seared by seeing loved ones die in the crematoria of Dachau and Buchenwald, they sought jobs in America and an opportunity to begin again. After World War II, the Displaced Persons Act and the Refugee Act helped about half a million newcomers into this country.

The Hungarians who were permitted to enter the United States when the Soviet Union crushed the Hungarian Revolution of 1956 had similar difficulties and sought similar opportunities as did refugees from Hitler's Germany. Most of the later immigrants, because of their relatively fewer numbers and the greater skills they brought with them, did not seek the ghettoes of the cities but became a more independent and dispersed group.

Those who sought political safety in the United States, as did immigrants from Germany and Hungary, did not in the main follow the patterns of adjustment established by earlier immigrant groups.

Because they were white in color and relatively few in number, they were gradually absorbed into the mainstream of American society. They sometimes brought important industrial skills or eagerly learned new ones. They worked, and in time they prospered. Today it is the newest newcomer, the Puerto Rican and the Negro, whose problems and patterns of adjustment resemble most closely those of the older immigrant.

How Did Puerto Ricans Come to the City?

The early newcomers, we have already noted, were immigrants. The later newcomers to the city were migrants. A migrant may be defined as one who leaves one part of a country and settles in another part of that same country. As the flow of immigrants to the city ebbed, the flow of migrants to the city increased. One source of migrants was the island of Puerto Rico.

As a result of the Spanish-American War, Puerto Rico was given to the United States by the Treaty of Paris in 1898. In 1900 the Congress of the United States established a government for the island. In 1917 the Puerto Ricans were granted citizenship by the Jones Act. As American citizens, Puerto Ricans could migrate freely from Puerto Rico to the mainland of the United States and back again whenever they chose to do so.

As a result of better living conditions resulting from the new prosperity that American business brought, the death rate on the island fell. Population grew rapidly; over-population and overcrowding became grave problems. Largely cancelled were whatever gains improved health and sanitary facilities made possible. For the masses, living conditions on the island became even harsher than they were before. Jobs were few and festering slums gave rise to disease and despair. The future of Puerto Rico and for Puerto Ricans looked bleak indeed. Under the leadership of Governor Luis Muñoz Marín and with the encouragement of the United States, conditions gradually improved. Nevertheless, for most Puerto Ricans conditions on the island were such that even the worst slum in America seemed to offer some hope and a chance at a better life. America's mainland seemed to offer possibilities for better living, greater prosperity, and above all, jobs. The search for jobs, more than anything else, best explains why Puerto Ricans came to the mainland. Fifty dollars for a plane ticket and six hours in the air brought them to New York.

While the search for jobs may be regarded as the major cause of Puerto Rican migration from the island, other factors were also at work. Many Puerto Ricans served in the armed forces in World War II and in the Korean War and began to enjoy the relatively high living standards that they found in army life as compared with island life. Television pictured in vivid detail the "good life" that was led by the prosperous in America. This too tempted Puerto Ricans to come. "And, as the Puerto Rican population of New York itself grew, and migrants and their children went back and forth by cheap airplane, everyone had direct personal knowledge of what life was like in New York. Once the stream is started and the road open, once the path is made easy, any minor cause will be sufficient to decide to try one's luck in New York: a poor marriage, overbearing parents, a sense of adventure, a desire to see New York itself."[6] The better schools, hospitals, and the welfare services of the city also played a role

There are over one-and-a-half million Puerto Ricans in the United States. About one-third of them are second generation. (Nathan Farb)

in attracting the Puerto Ricans to the city. However, one official remarked, "We know exactly when there's to be a recession on the mainland. We have only to watch the Puerto Ricans come back here. They are the last to be hired and the first to be fired, and if a slump is coming they know it right away."[7]

Most Puerto Rican migrants come to the United States in hopes of making money and then returning to their home in Puerto Rico. Because the island is near and the travel easy, the decision to leave Puerto Rico is not quite so grave as it was for the European immigrant who had to journey over 3,000 miles to come to America. For the European immigrant, the decision to leave his homeland usually meant a permanent break.

Some Puerto Ricans find excellent opportunities in the United States and bring their families and make permanent homes here. Others would like to go back, but indebtedness for furniture, televisions, and appliances forces some to remain against their will. Still others continue to make frequent trips from the mainland to the island and back again. Increasingly, however, while the tide of migration from Puerto Rico is not so great as it once was, those who come plan to stay, to work, and to contribute to the growth and welfare of the city.

How Did the Negro Come to the City?[8]

The movement of Negroes toward the cities of the North began to gain momentum early in the twentieth century. Events of the 1920's speeded up that movement. Because of World War I, Northern industry was rapidly expanding. But the world conflict had ended the flow of European immigrants upon which industry depended to fill its need for workers. Industry in the Northern cities now turned to the black migrant from the South to fill these positions. Labor recruiters, newspaper advertisements, letters, and personal contacts lured the Negro northward. The city denied the Negro first-class restaurants or hotels in which to eat or sleep. Only inferior jobs were available to him, yet those jobs were often better in the North than in the South. Of Chicago in the 1920's the singer Mahalia Jackson has this to say:

". . . In Chicago the colored world was in full bloom. Never before had Negroes lived so well or had so much money to spend. I'll never forget what a joy it was to see them driving up and down Southern Parkway and Michigan Boulevard in big, shiny touring cars and strolling in the evening, laughing and talking and calling out happily to each other."[9]

At about the same time that Northern industry lured the Negro away from the South, the boll weevil's destruction of the cotton farms drove him away and gave impetus to the Negro migration to Northern cities. Inferior and segregated schools and hospitals and humiliating social conditions further drove black men and women to the cities of the North. So great was the migration from the South between 1920 and 1930 that Georgia, for example, lost a total of one fourth of its black population over the age of ten. Most of the migrants were young adults. As in the case of most migrations, it is the young who do not feel bound to the existing system.

The Depression of the 1930's slowed migration as job opportunities in the North dried up. The flow resumed, however, as World War II created a great need for more manpower in Northern factories. This migration continued during the 1950's and 1960's and the cities of the West as well as those of the North gained in the number of non-white residents. Television depicted Northern life, and Southern blacks were interested in trying to see for themselves whether or not the opportunities they had seen on the TV screen and had heard about from others really existed. Cheap bus transportation made it increasingly possible for them to save enough money to buy a ticket, leave the place of their birth, and seek their fortune elsewhere.

The size of the Negro migration must not be exaggerated. Great though it was and great though it continues to be, it pales when compared with the earlier waves of European immigrants. Between 1901 and 1911 about 8.8 million immigrants came to America. Between 1960 and 1966, about 1.8 million more came. This is far greater than the 613,000 blacks who left the South during these years to settle in the large cities of the North and West. Nevertheless, this migration, though smaller than that of the immigrant migrations of the past, has altered the racial composition of large cities. In the South, as well as in the North, blacks have become a largely urbanized people. Central cities everywhere in America are becoming more heavily non-white. The core of any city is becoming mainly black in racial makeup. The twelve largest cities (New York, Chicago, Los Angeles, Philadelphia, Detroit, Baltimore, Houston, Cleveland, Washington, D.C., St. Louis, Milwaukee, and San Francisco) now contain over two thirds of the black population outside the South, or one third of the total black population in the United States. While migration may slow down somewhat, black population will continue to grow.[10] "As of 1966, the Negro population in all central cities totaled 12.1 million. By 1985 . . . it will rise 72% to 20.8 million . . . natural growth will account for 6 million of this increase and in-migration for 2.7 millions."[11]

The North to the Negro has become the "promised land," as Claude Brown put it. But for too many Negroes, the promises have yet to be kept. While New York's Harlem and Chicago's South Side may have been bright and prosperous places for the Negro during the 1920's, the Depression changed all that. The Depression hit the Negro hard, much harder than it did the white. Mahalia Jackson describes the changes that the Depression

wrought on the black community of Chicago during
the 1930's:

"When the Depression hit Chicago, the life Negroes had built for themselves in Chicago fell apart.
On the South Side it was as if somebody had pulled
a switch and everything had stopped running. Every
day another big mill or factory would lay off all its
colored help. Suddenly the streets were full of men
and women who'd been put out of their jobs. All
day long you'd see crowds of them shuffling back
and forth and standing on street corners. Banks all
over the South Side locked their doors and I'll never
forget seeing the long lines of people outside them
crying in the streets over their lost savings and fall-
ing on their knees and praying."[12]

The drab and sordid conditions of the black
ghettoes of the big cities, Harlem, Bedford-Stuyve-
sant, Watts, Hough, may all be said to have their
origins in segregation on the one hand and in the
Depression of the 1930's on the other. As the ghettoes of the central cities became increasingly grim,
whites moved farther and farther away. Today the
core of most large cities is a black ghetto. The
fringe of most large cities is inhabited by well-to-do
whites. These sharp contrasts between the rich and
the poor, the white and the black, the interests of
the suburb and those of the inner city, give rise to
tensions and to dangers which threaten the peace
and the lives of white and black alike. These tensions
threaten the fabric of urban life. They impair the
quality of life that can be lived in the city. Yet if the
city is the source of national strength, of cultural
achievement, and of economic growth, these tensions within the urban environment must be eased
lest the nation itself be destroyed.

The Negro and Puerto Rican newcomers migrated to the cities of the North for reasons similar to those of the earlier immigrants. They too looked for the security of living with a large group of their own people. The steamships of an earlier era deposited their human cargo of European immigrants at the docks of the large cities. The bus and train now pull into the terminals of the large cities bringing with them Southern, rural Negroes, while the airplane brings the Puerto Ricans to the cities of America, and especially to New York because it is the city that seems to offer the greatest number of jobs and the chance to earn a living. Lacking in modern industrial skills, the newcomers from Puerto Rico and from the South sought to take the unskilled jobs, often as dishwashers, houseworkers, rest room attendants, doormen, janitors, and the like. Because these jobs were among those easily eliminated by machines or otherwise abandoned in an economy on the move, the newcomers found themselves faced with periodic unemployment. Jobs in service industries (laundries, restaurants) were more plentiful than those in factories and there were more jobs available for women than for men. Because Negroes and Puerto Ricans were forced to accept marginal jobs, their patterns of adjustment to the city were and remain more varied than those of earlier newcomers. The process of becoming self-sufficient, of providing for themselves and their families, of taking part in the upward march of a rich nation has always been labored and slow.

How Did the Cities Receive the Newcomers?

The period between the Civil War and World War I was a time of great industrial change in the nation. The new factories needed a labor force and it was filled by millions of German, Scandinavian, Russian, Polish, Bohemian, Hungarian, Italian, Jewish, Oriental, and Irish immigrants. All of these newcomers were discriminated against in some degree. The immigrant was hated by those who feared their jobs would be taken away by newcomers willing to work for less money. Some older Americans were concerned about the crime rate that seemed to rise when newcomers entered the cities. Others had a general mistrust for people they did not understand because they spoke a foreign language, had different mannerisms, and were dressed in different garb. The way of life of the white, Protestant American seemed to be violated by the heavy-drinking Irish, the gangland antics of the Italians, and the supposed use of narcotics by the Orientals. Of course, just a few of the people in these groups were responsible for the things with which all of them were charged. Many political

For the old, there is no hope of leaving the ghetto, no hope of a better life. (Shalmon Bernstein). For the young, it is often hard to see beyond the walls of their confinement. (Arthur Tress)

leaders were Irish. The Italians and Orientals proved
to be hard-working, industrious people. But the il-
lusion was present, nonetheless. One by one these
groups showed their value to the city, but only after
a very difficult period of proving themselves, a
process which in many ways is a never-ending one.

Opportunities for the employment of the unskilled
laborers were not always equal to the great number
of immigrants who needed jobs. Because periods of
unemployment among immigrants were frequent, as
their numbers increased so too did the rate of pauperism, crime and delinquency. At least, so it
seemed. The problem of how to keep the newcomers fed and clothed and how to keep them from
getting into trouble with the law became very real
problems for city government. It also brought com-
plaints about the habits, life styles, and attitudes of
the newcomers. Even as early as 1819 when there
were relatively few immigrants entering New York
City, the manager of the Society for the Prevention
of Pauperism had this to say:

> "This country is the resort of vast numbers of
> these needy and wretched beings. . . . Many of them
> arrive here destitute of everything. . . . Instead of
> seeking the interior, they cluster in our cities, . . .
> depending on . . . charity, or depredation, for sub-
> sistence. . . . Many of these foreigners may have
> found employment; some may have passed into the
> interior; but thousands still remain among us. They
> are frequently found destitute in our streets; they
> seek employment at our doors; they are found in
> our almshouses, and in our hospitals; they are found
> at the bar of our criminal tribunals, in our . . . peni-
> tentiary, and our state prison. . . . They are too
> often led by want, by vice, and by habit . . . ren-

dering our city more liable to the increase of crimes,
and our houses of correction, more crowded with
felons."[13]

Nearly every immigrant group in every decade
in which they came had to overcome the indif-
ference or hostility of the older generation of Americans. The Jews faced economic and social barriers
which in great measure were traditional prejudices
the older generation of Americans had brought
with them from Europe. One New York newspaper
complained about the arrival of Italians in these
words:

"The flood gates are open. The bars are down.
The sally ports are unguarded. The dam is washed
away. The sewer is choked . . . the scum of immigration is . . . upon our shores. The hoard of . . .
steerage slime is being siphoned upon us from Con-
tinental mud tanks."[14]

The Irish also had to accept the injustices that
the American public had heaped upon them. Newspapers made special note that "no Irish need ap-
ply" for the jobs they advertised. Even the poetess
Emma Lazarus could not entirely veil a certain
superiority to the immigrant. The words, engraved
on the Statue of Liberty which stands in New York
Harbor, "Give me your tired, your poor, Your
huddled masses yearning to breathe free, The
wretched refuse of your teeming shore, Send these,
the homeless, tempest-tossed to me: I lift my lamp
beside the golden door," were not at all reassuring.
"The wretched refuse" could not be blamed if they
felt their welcome was less than warm.

Today the golden door is no more. In many ways

the Negroes and the Puerto Ricans have now taken
that place in our society that the immigrants previ-
ously held. The Negroes and Puerto Ricans of the
large city ghettoes are forced to live in substandard
dwellings. The ghetto is overcrowded, ridden with
crime and drug addiction. It has run-down, rat-
infested housing and a high infant death rate as well
as widespread mental, emotional and physical ill-
ness. There is conflict, violence, tension and friction
in the ghetto. But the ghetto also has young people,
black and Puerto Rican, who in spite of obstacles
get and hold good jobs, fight their way into college,
find a career, and make a good life for themselves.
Yet in relation to other groups that have found
themselves in a ghetto and at the bottom of the
social and economic ladder, the Negroes in our
larger cities should have left the slum and the
ghetto years ago. But the caste mark of a colored
skin has kept them where they are. The earlier newcomers, the Irish, Italian or Jew, could learn to
dress, and to speak, and to look like the older
American, but the Negro has the white-imposed
stigma of the color of his skin that he cannot hide.

Among Puerto Ricans, color as a factor in racial
discrimination is not great because more white than
black Puerto Ricans migrated to the mainland. However, when Puerto Ricans migrate to the mainland,
because they are Spanish-speaking and because their
skin color is darker than that of the older Americans
or European immigrants, they find themselves discriminated against just as much as the Negroes. For
them, such discrimination cuts very deep indeed.
Coming as they do from an island where they are
in the majority only to find that they are now a
scarcely tolerated minority hurts very much. In their
eagerness to "make it" in America, the white Puerto

The hope for a truly integrated non-discriminatory society is with the children who will grow up side-by-side with their black, Oriental, and Indian friends. (Joe Molnar)

Rican does not want to be taken for an American Negro, even though he may have a dark skin. The white and light-skinned Puerto Ricans are finding more rapid acceptance into American society, as did the immigrants before them. The darker-skinned Puerto Ricans find such acceptance much more difficult.[15]

Whether or not the blacks from the South and the Puerto Ricans will in due course have the chance to overcome the hostility toward newcomers that other migrants to the city faced is neither clear nor certain.

However, whatever progress or improvement in their social and economic condition they make will depend upon all the people of the city. The people of the city will "have to choose whether these newest arrivals are to be welcomed as equals or treated as enemies, whether they are to be given seats in the same schools and apartments in the same houses or excluded as foes to the existing order. . . . Much hangs on the character of that choice."[16]

How Did the Newcomers Fare in the Cities?

Distrust and prejudices were the "bitter pills" that each wave of immigrants had to swallow as they tried to make a better place for themselves and their families in the United States. It was not an easy task but each group helped meet the needs of American development and made their way to a better life.

The Irish were poor and unskilled when they arrived in overwhelming numbers. Contractors met them at the docks and they were usually hired for the building of canals and railroads. They also provided cheap labor for the New England mills and coal mines of Pennsylvania. As time went on the Irish pulled themselves up the economic and social ladder. They moved first into the field of law and then into politics and government. They speeded their assimilation by establishing their own churches, founding schools for their children, starting their own press, and by their labor leaders who fought to better the wages and working conditions of Irish workers.

The Germans were unique in the fact that most of them already had skills when they reached this country. They made their way up rather quickly in relation to other groups. They became teachers, engineers, scientists, artists. Many were prominent in bringing about government reform and improvement in the life of the cities. Carl Schurz, for example, was responsible for civil service reform, thus making merit rather than political favoritism the chief yardstick for political appointment.

The Italian immigrants followed much the same pattern of assimilation as the Irish did. They were untrained in special skills and had to rely on unskilled labor jobs to make a living. They became bricklayers, masons, stonecutters, and ditchdiggers. They worked on the railroads, in coal mines, iron mines, and factories. Some found a place in the city as small storekeepers, peddlers, shoemakers, barbers, and tailors. Their wives went into the needle trades. In time, most of the obstacles of prejudice and misunderstanding were overcome. Men like Angelo Patri and Leonard Covello became principals of public schools in New York City and in this capacity as educators sought to improve the lives of all newcomers who came to the community their schools served.

Not as many Orientals came into the United States as did those of other immigrant groups but they had to face even more prejudice from the American public than did the other groups. Because of their skin color and because of what appeared to be unusual mannerisms, they were referred to as the "yellow menace." They were often mobbed and stoned by native Americans. They were unskilled and were forced to take jobs that paid so little that even the wages of every member of the family were scarcely enough to support it. Even labor unions closed their membership to them. Despite such prejudice and perhaps because of it, Orientals, espe-

cially the Chinese, opened small businesses such as
restaurants and laundries and in this way served
the wider community and created employment for
their people.

The Jews were also faced with the problems of
securing whatever work they could find. They
established themselves in the needle trades as garment workers, hatmakers and furriers. These jobs
were done in vile sweat shops under foul, degrading
and dangerous conditions. They also became peddlers or opened small shops. More than most immigrant groups, Jews understood the importance of
getting an education, of learning English, and of
acquiring American citizenship. They sent their
children to day schools and flocked to night schools.
For them the free public school systems of the large
urban centers were a means of improving themselves. The children of peddlers became professional men and, while parents may have remained
behind, the children moved from the ghetto to the
better residential sections of the city and from there
to the prosperous suburbs.

Before 1900, the Negroes who came from the
South had a fairly good chance of succeeding. They
were barbers, waiters, caterers, and, in some cases,
skilled artisans, such as shoemakers or carpenters.
There was also a small business and professional
group among them. They were discriminated against,
to be sure, but the opportunity to make a decent
living was at least available.

In the 1920's, laws were passed severely reducing
the number of immigrants who could enter the
United States. Those who were here learned new
skills and moved upward from the lowest paying
jobs. These jobs were increasingly left for Negroes
to fill. Negroes were unable to pull themselves out

of the ghetto through their own efforts by starting small businesses and by employing those of their own race. Southern Negroes had little opportunity to have much experience with money and little opportunity to develop managerial skills. The close family ties that helped other immigrant groups did not exist among black Americans. Negro opportunity for self-employment and for self-help was limited. Other ethnic businessmen and professionals were able to count on the support of their own group. This the Negroes were unable to do. The cry of the Negro for "black power" is in part a demand for economic power in the form of help to start small businesses of their own. These businesses would cater to black customers, encourage black culture, and employ black workers in enterprises financed by black capital.

The Puerto Ricans, though following a pattern similar to that of the Negroes, appear to be making some headway in improving their economic and social status. However, the frequent trips of Puerto Ricans between the mainland and the island make it difficult to determine in which of the two social systems they wish to move. It may well be that the Puerto Rican community will not follow a pattern similar to that of other immigrant groups. Others essentially sought, and to a degree achieved, assimilation in the wider social environment of America. Not all Puerto Ricans appear to want to follow this pattern. Like the Chinese and Jews, the Puerto Ricans run a relatively large number of small businesses. The Puerto Rican shop owner supplies his community with the foods Puerto Ricans like to eat, the books they like to read, and the music they want to hear. One Puerto Rican organization, *Aspira,* is devoted to the job of helping Puerto

The upsurge in racial militancy among Negroes, American Indians, and Puerto Ricans, indicates a desperate attempt by these peoples to restore their feelings of inner strength, self-respect, and pride in their heritage; feelings which have long been concealed as a result of discrimination. *Below:* A black student take-over at Cornell University. *Opposite page top:* Puerto Rican leaders of the Young Lords after their take-over of an East Harlem church, used by them to run a breakfast program for ghetto children. *Opposite page bottom:* American Indians have taken over the abandoned prison island of Alcatraz off San Francisco's coast.

(Kay Krieghbaum, Black Star)

(UPI)

(Wide World)

Ricans follow the path to success taken by Jews
and Italians forty years ago. "It has a rather hope-
ful outlook, which emphasizes the group's potential
for achievement more than the prejudice and discrimination it meets. One can only hope that this
buoyant outlook will be better sustained by life in
the city. It is a note in tune with the gentleness and
gaiety of the Puerto Ricans themselves."[17]

Among the long-suffering immigrants to America
are the Mexican-Americans. Having long neglected
them, we are just now beginning to get some insight
into the incredible hardships and discrimination
under which they labor and to which they are subjected. Except for the American Indian, the Mexican-American has the oldest history in the New
World, although his acceptance by the American
people has yet to be achieved. The Mexican-American dominated the history of America's Southwest.
The American cowboy owes his know-how, his
folklore, and his skills to the traditions of the
Mexican-American.

Savagery against the Mexicans was common during the Mexican-American War (1846–1848). General Winfield Scott, who was commander of the
United States Army, complained of the widespread
and unnecessary murder and bloody atrocities com-
mitted by American troops on Mexican men, wom-
en, and children. Today Mexican-Americans form
an important source of unskilled labor for farms
and factories of the Southwest. Badly paid, ill-
housed, many migrant workers from Mexico are
illegal immigrants. Once the harvest is done and the
farmer has secured his crop, they are once again
driven back across the Rio Grande to Mexico. Stan
Steiner, in his book *La Raza,* refers to the area of
the Rio Grande valley as "The Region of the

Damned." Unlike most immigrants who seek their fortunes in the city, the Chicano (Mexican-American) tries to eke out his existence in rural poverty under conditions not far from peonage. When the work is over, or when their frustration becomes too great, many take off for the cities, usually Los Angeles. Poverty and racial discrimination hang over the Mexican-American with a special kind of intensity. Part of it stems from the fact that before the situation can be remedied it must first be exposed. This is just now beginning to happen.

How Do Immigrant and Migrant Experiences as Newcomers Compare?

As we have stated, an immigrant is someone who leaves the country of his birth to settle permanently in another; a migrant is someone who leaves one

Gentleness and gaiety. (Joe Molnar)

part of his country to settle in another part of the same country. Up to 1920, before immigration quotas reduced their number to a mere trickle, immigrants swelled the great cities of America. First they came from Northern and Western Europe and later from Southern and Eastern Europe. At about the time that the immigrant wave began to shrink, the migrant wave began to grow. Negroes from the South and Puerto Ricans from the island came in increasing numbers to settle in the cities. How do the experiences of these different waves of newcomers resemble or differ from each other?

In his book on this subject, Oscar Handlin writes, "The Negroes and Puerto Ricans have followed the general outline of the experiences of earlier immigrants."[18] The author expects that, by and large, both groups will follow the path of earlier newcomers in moving upward in the economic and social ladder. While prejudice against men of color may slow down the pace of such upward mobility, it cannot prevent it. The constant travel back and forth between Puerto Rico and the continent may also mean that Puerto Ricans may remain an unassimilated island of Spanish-speaking people. But for those who choose to stay, they too can expect to better themselves. Both for the black and for the Puerto Rican, however, economic and social improvement cannot come without massive help from private and government sources. Why should such help be given?

There are many reasons. They grow out of the different set of circumstances that faces the migrant of today as compared with the immigrant of yesterday. For one thing, today's migrant from the South is black, and many of those from Puerto Rico, while not black, nevertheless have a dark skin.

While men should be color-blind in extending economic and social opportunities, the sad fact remains that color has placed an enduring obstacle in the path of the cities' most recent arrivals. They cannot be expected to move upward unless they have the protection of laws which effectively open equal opportunity for them. With the exception of Asiatics, the immigrant of yesterday, whatever else was against him, such as language or country of origin, did not have the hurdle of a colored skin to overcome.

Moreover, while the immigrant came with relatively few skills, he came at a time when the American economy was such that it could absorb the unskilled with relative ease. Industry was bustling and essentially youthful. It was simple in many of its industrial methods. Although cruel in the demands that it made of its labor, it was the means which gave the immigrant a start. Even at its worst, it was somewhat better than the conditions under which the immigrant had lived and worked in his native land. No matter how low the wages, the immigrant was able to save, and bit by bit work and hope for better times.

Puerto Ricans and Negroes find conditions to be different. Unskilled labor is not so desperately needed. Industry is older now and industrial methods are such that a wide variety of simple and even complex tasks can be done by machines. Muscle power alone cannot earn for the Negro and Puerto Rican the livelihood it earned for the immigrant. Because unions protect salaries and working conditions for labor, the most recent newcomer, unlike those of the past, cannot offer to work for lower wages. Unions have also made it difficult for blacks or Puerto Ricans to join, thus denying them job opportunities. Only government laws have forced some unions to open their membership to the migrant newcomers.

The immigrant of old was mainly urban in character. When he moved from Europe to America he often moved from a simple urban environment to a larger and more complicated one. In this process of uprooting himself he essentially never left the city. The process of adjustment was in this sense somewhat easier. His close family and religious ties helped him. Successful men from the country of his birth reached down and lent a helping hand. The local political machines, in exchange for the immigrant's vote, encouraged him to become a citizen, provided jobs, and helped him when disaster struck.

The black and Puerto Rican migrants come mainly from rural environments. For them, adjustment to the city life is difficult, to say the least. Those who take the train or bus and travel hundreds of miles to reach the city, find it all but hopeless to use the cities' subways or bus lines properly. They do not readily locate those government services that can offer help in finding a job or in applying for assistance. At best, the pace and impersonality of the city are bewildering. At worst, the city aggravates the feelings of inferiority with which they come. Although both blacks and Puerto Ricans are citizens, both had to overcome discriminatory voting laws which made the right to vote seem like a special privilege. Both groups had few family ties to help them, few successful models to follow, and few successful businessmen with jobs to offer.

Despite these handicaps and these differences, what deserves to be emphasized is not how few have "made it" but rather how many. While more

These women have successfully worked out a balance of old world and new. (Arthur Tress)

should make it and faster, nevertheless the American dream is still appropriate. What the American economy made possible for the immigrant must be made possible for the Negro and Puerto Rican. But for the dream to be realized new approaches to problems of urban poverty will have to be developed.

What Did Newcomers Contribute to Our Cities and Our Country?

Wherever one turns, one finds the impact of the immigrant. For instance, if one turns to the American dinner table, one can see the influence that the newcomer has made upon our society. Lasagna, chile con carne, sauerkraut, Irish stew, Welsh rarebit, English muffins, Gruyère cheese, Danish pastry, filet mignon, chop suey, gefilte fish, hominy grits and collard greens are some of the "typical American dishes" one may find served on any table in any home.

If one turns to government in America, there too newcomers helped to form the nation's political structure. Out of the fifty-six signers of the Declaration of Independence, eighteen were of non-English stock and eight were first generation immigrants. Each immigrant group, in fighting for social acceptance, economic opportunity, and political freedom, fought for all as well as for each. The democratizing influence of the newcomer helped to extend the vote and broaden popular government. We are now in the midst of a social revolution as the newcomers from the South, from Puerto Rico, and from south of the border seek acceptance, opportunity, and power. There is no assurance that the black, Puerto Rican, and Mexican newcomers will also "overcome," as did those before them. We do know, however, that no advances can be achieved without a struggle. Their victory, if it comes, will not be theirs alone but will be shared with the rest of American society.

For many immigrants, America was the land in which they hoped to seek their fortune. While very few really did find the fortune they sought, some of those who did are noteworthy examples of what was possible. Among those are Andrew Carnegie (Scot) in the steel industry, John Jacob Astor (German) in the fur trade, the DuPonts (French) of the munitions and chemical industry, and Charles Fleischmann (Hungarian) of the yeast business.

Some of the many scientists and inventors who were among the newcomers may be cited here: Albert Einstein (German) in physics; Enrico Fermi (Italian) in atomic research; John Ericsson (Swedish) who invented the screw propeller and the ironclad ship; Igor Sikorsky (Russian) who contributed to the development of the airplane; and Alexander Graham Bell (Scot) who invented the telephone.

While it is well known that George Washington Carver, a Negro, developed nearly three hundred different products from the peanut, the contributions of other black men have long been neglected. Norbert Rillieux of Louisiana invented a sugar refining process, while in Detroit, Elijah McCoy had fifty-seven different patents to his credit, some of which were used in steamships and railroads and others were useful in telegraphy. Benjamin Banneker was a first-rate astronomer, while Jan E. Matzeliger's new invention led to mass production of shoes in America. Dr. Daniel Hale Williams developed a blood plasma bank and anticipated the heart

Bocce courts, built by the city, bring a bit of old Italy to the community and draw Italians together. (Anthony Mazzariello)

transplant operations of modern times. A list of Negro "greats" in medicine, invention, and industry would fill more space than is available, as those mentioned here are but representative of the quality of the black man's contribution to America.

Puerto Ricans have also made their mark in many walks of life. José Ferrer and Juano Hernandez are noted for their fine acting, Graciela Singer has entertained America as a singer, while Ruben Gomez, Juan Pizzaro and Jim Rivera are among the outstanding Puerto Rican baseball players. In politics too Puerto Ricans have risen to positions of prominence. Carlos Rios serves in the government of New York City as a councilman and Herman Badillo is a successful New York lawyer and politician. Felipe Torres and Manuel Gomez serve as judges.

Is the City a Melting Pot?

In 1782, Jean de Crèvecoeur, in his *Letters from an American Farmer,* said that in the United States "individuals of all nations are melted into a new race of men." Since that time our country has often been referred to as a "melting pot." But nothing could be farther from the truth. The immigrants and migrants were not "melted into a new race of men." Each remained distinct individuals who brought with them characteristics and mores that were almost impossible to melt away in a few generations. When we look at immigrant living patterns, we find that every large city has its Italian, Jewish, Polish, Negro, Spanish, Chinese, Puerto Rican, and German neighborhoods. In these neighborhoods can be found the food, religion, and language of the country or the area from which they or their families came. Even the first and second generation Americans not only retain their ethnic ties, but even strengthen them in defense against groups of other and perhaps older immigrants.

In their book, *Beyond the Melting Pot,* Nathan Glazer and Daniel Patrick Moynihan point out that even after distinctive language and culture customs are lost, ethnic groups continue to have a life of their own.[19] Men are connected with the ethnic group into which they were born by ties of family and friends. One's very name may have a Jewish, Irish, or Italian ring which places him in the ethnic group of which he is a part, no matter how far from the original characteristics of such a group he may have strayed. Moreover, the authors point out, such ethnic groups are not merely ethnic. Instead, they are interest groups as well. That is, each of these groups has certain interests of its own for which it fights. This may be the abolition of discrimination in housing, or more jobs, or better schools. Each group then has not only ethnic and family ties but has common demands to extract from society. These common demands make and keep the groups distinctive from one another.

Today as never before, the people of the city are faced with tensions. In part these spring from the conflict between the rich and poor and between the white and the black. These tensions are also in part the result of conflict between the desires of the older immigrant (Jew, Italian, Irish) to protect what he has worked so hard to win, and the black, Puerto Rican, and Mexican newcomers who have been waiting far too long for economic and social improvement. Migrants, old and new, clash in housing, in education, and in rivalry for jobs. Such

Many different ethnic groups parade down Fifth Avenue in New York, adding their spirit to the city. The St. Patrick's Day Parade is the most famous. (UPI)

conflict is not new. To the extent that the interests
of one race are different from those of another, conflict is to be expected. One may even say that such
conflict is healthy if the means used to resolve it
are peaceful. When, however, such conflict degen-
erates into race hatred, when violence is used to
crush opposition, then the danger becomes great.
Religion and race are two elements which determine
the group to which a person belongs. Had America
really "melted," religion and race would be unim-
portant factors in the life of urban America. Instead,
they are vitally important factors in the political,

These Ku Klux Klansmen
don't spread race hatred
through the South. This
meeting took place in Dearborn, Michigan, February 1,
1970. (UPI)

economic, and social life of any city. It will take men of good will on all sides to prevent the clash of interests from becoming a clash of race or religion.

"The American in abstract does not exist."[20] Instead, what we have are the people of the city. Each person comes from a distinctive racial, religious, or ethnic stock. Each is more or less a newcomer to the city. Each, despite the passage of time, remains closely tied to the roots from which he sprang. As those roots deepen, as his hold on urban America becomes more secure, he becomes proud of his na-

tional origin. The people then are not only of the city. Instead they are of many communities—racial, national, ethnic—each contributing to all the drives, ambitions, temper that make the city what it is and what it deserves to be.

Part Two

Selected Readings

Bride and Groom, by Amedeo Modigliani. (Collection, The Museum of Modern Art, New York. Gift of Frederic Clay Bartlett.)

While all Americans are immigrants or descendants of immigrants, the white, Anglo-Saxon Protestants (WASPS) have for generations dominated the social, economic, political, and cultural life of the nation. Today in American cities, while the "Establishment" continues to be powerful, it is a distinct minority and, if it is to retain power, must compete with other minorities for it. In the selection which follows we see how Lincoln's family became members of the Establishment during the 19th century and the factors that are contributing to the decline of the Establishment during the 20th century.

1

The Protestant Establishment

by E. DIGBY BALTZELL

WHILE Abraham Lincoln's own career has been a well-publicized example of the democratic ideal of individual opportunity, the career of his son Robert Todd Lincoln was an equally instructive example of the less-publicized but no less important aristocratic process. Abraham Lincoln himself was well aware of the importance of the aristocratic process, first when he married into an established family in the Middle West and then when he sent

From *The Protestant Establishment*, by E. Digby Baltzell (New York: Random House, 1964), pp. 10–15, 229–32. Copyright © 1964 by E. Digby Baltzell. Reprinted by permission of Random House, Inc., and Martin Secker & Warburg, Ltd.

his son Todd to the Phillips Academy, in Exeter, New Hampshire, in order that he be educated in the style of the Eastern Seaboard upper class.

After finishing his education at Harvard College and the Law School, and after his marriage to the beautiful and fashionable daughter of Senator James Harlan, Robert Todd Lincoln went on to become one of the nation's leading corporation lawyers, a multimillionaire, and a typical Victorian aristocrat. He and his family lived at the very core of the upper class in Chicago as well as in New York and Washington. In addition to his proper education and famous family connections, his secure membership in the new, and national, associational upper class which grew up in America in the closing decades of the nineteenth century was nicely indicated by his club affiliations. An early Social Register, for example, listed his memberships in New York's patrician Union and more intellectual Century clubs, the Chicago Club in Chicago, and the Metropolitan and Chevy Chase clubs in Washington. For many years, the "Bob Lincoln Corner" at the Metropolitan was a famous gathering place for good conversation and humor.

Robert Todd Lincoln made every effort not to trade on his father's name and sedulously avoided publicity. In one of his few speeches in memory of his father he emphasized his own faith that "in our country there are no ruling classes." Yet he was constantly in demand in a crude, plutocratic age which longed for the stable authority of tradition. Too shy and retiring to run for public office, he nevertheless served when called, in the aristocratic tradition, as a devoted and conservative Republican in the cabinets of Garfield and Arthur and as Minister to the Court of St. James under Harrison. In

Chicago, where he made his home for many years, he was referred to as the "Prince of Rails" and became the nearest thing to royal authority the raw young city possessed. He was not only sought after by the fashionable, the plutocratic and the powerful in this country, many of whom, like Andrew Carnegie, he counted among his friends; he was also in demand abroad, where he was entertained by Queen Victoria and many other leaders; and of course important visitors to this country, like Lloyd George,* sought him out as a symbol of the best American traditions.

Robert Todd Lincoln lived the life of a typical Victorian aristocrat in an age when his class led the nation and dominated its traditions. He was at the height of his business career as president of the George M. Pullman Company as the Victorian Age waned with the death of the Queen in 1901. In that year a British-American, White–Anglo–Saxon–Protestant (WASP) establishment, consolidated through family alliances between Mayfair and Murray Hill involving many millions of dollars, authoritatively ran the world, as their ancestors had done since Queen Elizabeth's time. . . .

At this point, it is well to emphasize that the aristocratic process worked quite well, and was taken for granted, throughout most of the nineteenth century, largely because the WASP upper class was still representative in an era when the vast majority of leaders, like Abraham Lincoln, were of old-stock origins anyway. Even the few exceptions, such for example as the brilliant Jew August Belmont, were assimilated the more easily because they constituted such a small minority.

Lloyd George—former Prime Minister of England.

The transition from the twenties to the thirties, from Hoover to Roosevelt, from Wall Street to Washington, and, above all, from a business-dominated to a government-dominated society was indeed a social revolution of major proportions. The immediate cause, of course, was the collapse of the economy and the Great Depression. But the revolutionary mood of the thirties was also the product of other social forces which had been gaining momentum throughout the first three decades of the century. Of importance here were the following: (1) between 1900 and 1930 the majority of American people came to live in cities; (2) while old-stock Protestants still dominated rural America, ethnic heterogeneity marked the city; (3) the newer immigrants who came to America after 1880 were predominantly urban dwellers; (4) because of the shortage of labor during the First War as well as the closing of the gates to cheap labor from overseas immediately afterward, Negroes and poor-whites from the South migrated to our large urban industrial areas in the North; (5) and finally, the children of these migrants to the urban frontier, educated in the public schools, slowly improved their economic position and sought to take their place in the political life of the nation as they came of age in the thirties. In other words, the political reforms instituted by the New Deal in order to bring the nation as a whole out of the Great Depression were, at the same time, strongly supported by the members of racial and ethnic minority groups, the vast majority of whom were still to be found at the lowest levels of the economic pyramid. The economic battle to liquidate the Depression was fused with the minority battle to liquidate both the heritage of slavery and the second-class status of the hyphen-

ated American. And the Northern wing of the
Democratic Party, which had been kept alive ever
since the Civil War by the political machines run by
the sons of Irish immigrants, now became the party
of the whole urban melting pot, made up of Poles,
Italians, Jews and Czechs as well as the swelling
tide of deracinated* Negroes and hillbillies from the
South. Just as Andrew Jackson had once trans-
formed the Democrats into majority status as the
hero of the Scotch-Irish immigrants to the Middle
Western frontier (often referred to as "foreign sav-
ages" and "liars" by members of the resentful Fed-
eralist establishment), so Franklin Roosevelt became
the hero, as Samuel Lubell has put it, of the hetero-
geneous mass of new arrivals on the Urban Frontier.

FURTHER INQUIRY

1. Former President Kennedy, although Catholic, may be considered as one who was
   part of the Establishment. What is the role
   of religion in making one part of or keeping
   one out of the Establishment?
2. Is there a Jewish Establishment? A Catholic
   Establishment?
3. The college one attends and the clubs one is
   permitted to join are among the ties that
   make the Establishment possible. How important are these institutions in creating
   and molding a ruling class?
4. Is America a classless society?
5. Does an aristocracy have a place in America? What should that place be? What cri-
   teria for membership should be established?

---

deracinated—uprooted.

Morrie Turner, a black cartoonist, received his first inspiration to create an integrated comic strip from Charles Schulz, the originator of "Peanuts." Later, Turner discussed the idea with comedian and civil rights leader Dick Gregory. Today Turner's "Wee Pals" is carried by more than thirty-two newspapers here and abroad.

2

Wee Pals

by MORRIE TURNER

From *Wee Pals*, by Morrie Turner (New York: New American Library, 1969), pp. 11, 17, 29. Copyright © 1969 by The Register and Tribune Syndicate, Inc. Reprinted by permission of The Register and Tribune Syndicate, Inc.

71

This selection, written by a Swedish scholar, describes the perils of a steerage passage aboard a ship during the nineteenth century. The author says that the suffering endured was greater than that on a slave ship.

3

The Notorious
Steerage

by EINAR J. ANDERSON

THE overcrowding of the immigrant ships has always been one of the chief causes for much of the attendant hardships. Throughout the various countries agents of shipping companies sold passage to immigrants without keeping any record of the total number of sales for a certain boat. Usually more tickets were sold than the ship could ac-

From "The Voyage of the Immigrant and How It Has Changed," by Einar J. Anderson, *Swedish-American Historical Bulletin*, Vol. II, No. 3, August, 1929, pp. 77–85. Reprinted by permission of the Swedish-American Historical Collection, Minnesota Historical Society.

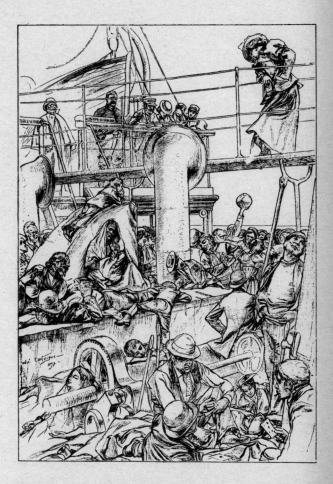

Steerage passage marked the beginning of hardship, misery and unsanitary conditions which many new immigrants had to face as they began their new life in America. (New York Public Library Picture Collection)

commodate in the steerage, and they were either
crowded on or left to wait for the departure of the
next boat. This exposed the disappointed emigrant
to further expense and exploitation. Often the steamship company had sold its steerage space for a certain sum, and it was then left to the immigrant
company to pack into the quarters as many as it
could hold; and while out on the high seas neither
party could be held responsible for the intense suffering. . . .

The medical examinations given before embark-
ing as well as those on the boat were merely perfunctory,* to live up to the letter and not the intention of the law. No passenger was spared the ill
treatment by the porters in boarding the boat nor
the filthy and blasphemous words heaped upon them
throughout the long thirty-seven days of the journey.
A few years previous, it had been customary for
each passenger to provision himself, but so few had
laid in large enough stores for the trip, that the
Hamburg and Bremen lines started a policy, followed soon by the other lines, of the ships supply-
ing the rations every week. This did away with the
starvation so common before. . . .

When the steerage passengers came to get their
water allowance, sixty were served and then the
crew announced that no more would be issued before the following day. The weekly food allowance
was not given out before the fifth day, which caused
a great deal of suffering as many who were poor
did not take any food along, depending upon the
terms of the contract. Even though children sixteen
years of age and under were to be considered as
full passengers, they were listed as children so as to

------

perfunctory—careless.

Ellis Island was the first stop for the early immigrants. Here papers were checked, and immigrants were given clothes and food. But if quotas from a country were filled, or papers were not in order, Ellis Island was the only part of America that some travelers saw before being shipped back to their home country. (Wide World)

serve them only half rations. Only one-half of the provisions that had been promised were issued during the trip. Handling the 900 members of the steerage was considered only a sideline of the ship's crew.

Each passenger was given a ticket which entitled him to cook one meal a day on the ship's range, but anyone would have been lucky to get one meal cooked in two days. There was such a demand for the one stove that those too poor to tip the steward would never get their chance in the waiting line. The doctor also demanded tips for any service rendered. When a child died from lack of nourishment, he was sewn in a sack and lowered into the sea without any ceremony.

Similar conditions prevailed at the time of the famine in Ireland, when so many of the weakened and undernourished people took passage for the United States or Canada. The suffering endured was greater than on any slave ship and the death rate was greater than from any plague or pestilence on shore. The food dealt out to them was poor, mostly a cheap grade of Indian corn, much of which was spoiled. There was always a scarcity of water and on one Irish ship headed for New York in 1847 they nearly ran out of food and water when only half of the trip had been completed. Soon many suffered from ship fever which in turn developed into cholera. The people were usually so crowded and the air so poisoned that usually upon arrival one-half of the passengers would remain below in a helpless condition. Many had been in bed for several days without the slightest attempt to care for them. Carrying doctors on board was not compulsory. Upon opening the hatches, the health officers were frequently compelled to have the fire-engine pump started, that by means of a stream of water the deadly atmosphere between decks, very much like that in a coal pit, might be sufficiently purified to render comparatively safe the undertaking of moving those below.

During the year 1847 the number of Irish emigrants leaving for Canada, according to the report of the chief secretary for Ireland, was 89,783. Of these 6100 died at sea, 4100 died upon arrival and 7100 shortly afterwards in hospitals. Although some of these deaths may be attributed to the weakened conditions in which many entered upon the voyage, the part played by the steerage cannot be ignored. The ships were not fit for transporting livestock, let alone human beings.

· · ·

Male and female, young and old were thus thrown together with only narrow boards separating them into stalls or arbitrary compartments. This purely imaginary separation of classes was done to aid circulation of air, these decks being at least twelve feet below the water line. No attempt was made to force air or ventilate by a mechanical process.

The situation was unspeakable, particularly when seasickness attacked the majority of the occupants, and the presence of perhaps fifty small children added to the discomfort. Most ships had compartments for single women, but since the air was worse there, they soon joined the rest in the general rooms. Often when cholera, smallpox, and typhus broke out, it was very difficult to keep them from spreading with a rapidity and violence of a Chicago fire. The lack of good air, unsanitary habitations, crowded conditions, and poor food, often exhausted several days before arrival, only tended to encourage disease. . . .

The few washrooms were small and dirty and not always on the same deck where the steerage were quartered. Only salt water was used, and the hot water in one faucet was soon monopolized, as this was the only place on the ship where warm water could be secured for washing individual dishes. No soap or towels were furnished. In many cases reported there were no separate washrooms for men and women. Many avoided the washrooms by stealing some water during the day or saving on their allotted drinking water and keeping it in small wine flasks. In the mornings they would try to wash while sitting in their berths and ignore the prying eyes of those about them.

. . .

The old style steerage was . . . injurious to
health [and] . . . Congress finally took the matter
seriously in hand and made sweeping changes in
the laws pertaining to that part of the immigrants'
voyage, referred to as the steerage.

FURTHER INQUIRY

1. What legislation, if any, was needed to
   remedy steerage conditions?
2. Why was delay in getting steerage accom-
   modation often the biggest disappointment
   of all?

In 1831, a group of 53 Norwegians
crossed the Atlantic in a sloop, "The Re-
sistance," a ship one-fourth the size of
the "Mayflower," which had brought the
first immigrants to New England over
200 years before. The ship was the first
of the Norwegian "sloopers" which came
between 1825 and 1835. The letter
below shows the great enthusiasm the
early settlers felt for their new land.

4

The "Sloopfolk" Arrive

edited by THEODORE C. BLEGEN

From Gjert G. Hovland, at Kendall Settlement,*
New York, to Torjuls A. Maeland

Kendall Settlement—a settlement of Norwegians.

From *Land of Their Choice*, edited by Theodore C. Blegen
(Minneapolis: University of Minnesota Press, 1955), pp. 19–29.
Copyright © 1955 by University of Minnesota.

April 22, 1835

I must take this opportunity to let you know that
we are in the best of health, and that both my wife
and I are exceedingly well satisfied. Our son attends the English school and talks English as well
as the native-born. Nothing has made me more
happy and contented than that we left Norway and
came to this country. We have gained more since
our arrival here than I did during all the time I
lived in Norway, and I have every prospect of
earning a living here for myself and my family
—even if my family becomes larger—so long as
God gives me good health.

Such excellent plans have been developed here
that, even though one be infirm, no one need go
hungry. Competent men are elected to see that no
needy persons, either in the cities or in the country,
shall have to beg. If a man dies and leaves a widow
and children who are unable to support themselves
—as often happens—they have the privilege of
petitioning these officials. Each one will then re-
ceive every year as much clothing and food as he
needs, and no discrimination is shown between the
native-born and those from foreign countries. These
things I have learned through daily observation, and
I do not believe there can be better laws and ar-
rangements for the benefit and happiness of the
common man in the whole world. I have talked
with a sensible person who has traveled in many
countries, who has lived here twenty-six years, and
has full knowledge of the matter; I asked both him
and other reliable persons, for I wish to let everyone know the truth.

When assemblies are held to elect officials to
serve the country, the vote of the common man

carries just as much authority and influence as that of the rich and powerful man. Neither in the matter of clothes nor in manners are distinctions noticeable, whether one be a farmer or a clerk. The one enjoys just as much freedom as the other. So long as he comports himself honestly he meets no interference. Everybody is free to travel about in the country, wherever he wishes, without passports or papers. Everyone is permitted to engage in whatever business he finds most desirable, in trade or commerce, by land or by water. But if anyone is found guilty of a crime, he is prosecuted and severely punished.

No duties are levied upon goods that are produced in the country and brought to the city by land or by water. In case of death, no registration is required; the survivor, after paying the debts, is free to dispose of the property for himself and his family just as he pleases. There is no one here who snatches it away, like a beast of prey, wanting only to live by the sweat of others and to make himself heir to the money of others. No, everyone must work for his living here, whether he be of high or low estate. It would greatly please me to learn that all of you who are in need and have little chance of supporting yourselves and your families have decided to leave Norway and come to America; for, even if many more come, there will still be room here for all. Those who are willing to work will not lack employment or business here. It is possible for all to live in comfort and without want.

. . .

We left our home in Norway on June 24, 1831. Sailing from Gothenburg on July 30, we landed in America September 18, and by October 4 we had reached this place in the interior where we now

live. The day after my arrival I began to work for
an American. In December I bought myself fifty
acres of land. I put up a house which we moved
into in the month of March 1832. I then set to
work with the greatest will and pleasure, for the
land was covered with trees. In the fall I planted
about one barrel of wheat, and in the spring of
1833 we planted about half a bushel of Indian corn
and three bushels of potatoes (the latter in May).
The next fall we harvested 15 barrels of wheat, 6
barrels of Indian corn, and 14 barrels of potatoes. . . .

Six families of the Norwegians who had settled
in this place sold their farms last summer and
moved farther west in the country to a place called
Illinois. We and another Norwegian family also
sold our farms and intend to journey, this May, to
that state, where land can be bought at a better
price, and where it is easier to get started. There
are only enough trees there to meet actual needs.
Cattle can be fed there at little cost, for one can
cut plenty of hay. The United States owns an un-
told amount of land which is reserved by law at a
set price for the one who first buys it from the
government. It is called public land and is sold
for $1.25 per acre. Land thus bought and paid for
is held in alodial* possession for the purchaser and
his heirs. Whether native-born or foreign, a man is
free to do with it whatever he pleases.

This is a beautiful and fertile country. Prosperity
and contentment are almost everywhere. Practically
everything needed can be sown or planted here and
grows splendidly, producing a yield of manyfold
without the use of manure.

---

alodial—without further rent.

Scandanavians, especially, preferred to leave the city once they had arrived in the new land. They were mostly farmers and many settled in the Midwest. (The Jacob A. Riis Collection, Museum of the City of New York)

Law and order exist here, and the country is governed by wise authorities.

    .   .   .

In America you associate with good and kindly people. Everyone has the freedom to practice the teaching and religion he prefers. The only tax a man pays here is on the land he owns, and even that tax is not large. Nor are there other useless expenditures for the support of persons—as in many places in Europe—who are of more harm than benefit to the country. For the fifty acres I sold I paid a dollar a year in taxes. On the piece of land we sold there were more trees than I could count of that kind that produces sugar, and these trees were common everywhere. We took no more than we needed for our own use each year. . . .

There is much more I could write to you about, but I will close for this time, with hearty greetings from me and my wife and son to you, my relatives, and acquaintances.

FURTHER INQUIRY

1. What are your impressions of the relative prosperity of the "sloopers" as compared with your impressions of later immigrants?
2. Does this letter paint an unduly bright picture of the new arrival's lot in America?
3. The letter was widely read in Norway. What impact do you think it made?

The author describes a special group of German immigrants who came to America in 1848 following unsuccessful revolutions in Germany. Should an immigrant with "revolutionary" ideas be kept out of America? Is it right for an immigrant to support revolutionary causes in the land of his birth?

5

The Forty-Eighters

by THEODORE HUEBENER

AMERICA, the land of the free and the home of the brave! The young democracy across the ocean exerted an unusual attraction on the minds of the Forty-Eighters. Well-educated, they had read widely and knew de Tocqueville* and the reports of German travelers in the States. Americans had

Alexis de Tocqueville—a well-known French writer who described America as he saw it in the 1830's. He is the author of *Democracy in America*.

From *The Germans in America*, by Theodore Huebener (Philadelphia: Chilton Company, 1962), pp. 95–103. Copyright © 1962 by The Center for Curriculum Development, Inc. Reprinted by permission of The Center for Curriculum Development, Inc.

established free democratic institutions. Their magnificent land was expanding and prospering. Furthermore, many of the Forty-Eighters were poetically and romantically inclined. They were fascinated by the glorious forests and the noble Indian as portrayed by Chateaubriand. Yes, America was the promised land.

It is very difficult, in fact impossible, to provide any accurate figures of the number of Forty-Eighters that came to the United States. Many of them came as individuals. Some came for a brief visit and returned later. At most, they amounted to a few thousand who were entirely lost in the huge wave of German immigration between 1846 and 1856. Some of the revolutionaries came before 1848, some years later. It is their political attitude, rather than the date of their arrival, by which they can be classified.

What was the reaction of the Germans in America to what was going on in the land of their birth? It seems that the earlier German immigrants took little interest in politics. They had come here for better living conditions and were satisfied with the opportunity to provide a comfortable livelihood for their families. They relished the free air of democracy and had absolutely no use for the autocratic princes who ruled the Fatherland. German-American sentiment, as reflected in the German language newspapers and magazines of the day, was unequivocally* on the side of the revolutionists. No one raised his voice in defense of kings and queens, and many editors demanded a German republic. The possible advent of a truly democratic and united Germany was hailed with elation. Emotions

---

unequivocally—without doubt.

Many of the German immigrants in the early 19th century were well educated and belonged to the middle or upper classes. (New York Public Library Picture Collection)

ran high. There were mass meetings, demonstrations of sympathy, parades and memorial services. In New York a great *Revolutionsfest* was held. Thousands of representatives from various ethnic groups marched down Broadway to a park, where Jakob Uhl, the publisher of *Staats-Zeitung,* presided at a huge meeting. Speeches were made in four foreign languages.

. . .

Hundreds of thousands of Germans had migrated to the United States, but no group made such an impact on the American scene as a few thousand Forty-Eighters. Although there had been some intellectuals among the earlier immigrants, the bulk of the Germans arriving in the United States before 1848 were peasants and tradesmen. The Forty-Eighters, on the other hand, were well-educated; by profession, they were generally teachers, doctors, lawyers, editors, artists, or musicians. It is no wonder, then, that they were able to create a sort of

89

intellectual renaissance among the German-American element.

There were other characteristics that distinguished the Forty-Eighters from the earlier German immigrant. He usually came alone; he was unencumbered by family and baggage. If he brought anything, it was a bag full of books and papers. He did not come directly from home; sometimes he had fled from an unsuccessful skirmish or had just gotten out of jail. Before he arrived in America, he had spent some time in England, France or Switzerland. He knew several languages, but little English. He was well-informed about political and social conditions in the United States. As a cultivated person, his chief interest was ideas and not the practical demands of life on the frontier.

It was natural that these differences caused a split between the old immigrants and the new. The former were referred to as the "Grays" *(Die Grauen)* and the newcomers as the "Greens" *(Die Grünen)*. The "Grays" admitted that they might not have had much booklearning, but they had cleared the land and built up prosperous farms and factories. They disliked the Forty-Eighters' radicalism, their criticism of American institutions, and their sarcastic comments on the low intellectual level of the German-Americans. In short, they detested the superior attitude of these "European beer politicians."

On the whole, the influence of the Forty-Eighters was salutary* on the German-Americans and on America as a whole. This was due to certain German traits which they all manifested, whether they belonged to the radical, moderate, or conservative wings of the revolution. The Forty-Eighters were primarily politically minded. They participated vig-

---

salutary—beneficial.

orously in the political life of their adopted land. This meant not patronage, but the maintenance of good government. With a Teutonic stubbornness they adhered to their principle, which was never sacrificed to party or personal expediency. They refused to "play the game"; they disdained the Anglo-Saxon tendency to compromise. They insisted on absolute truth, although this was quite impractical in any society of fallible human beings.

In this respect they were extremely conservative. They preferred the overbearing but uncorruptible bureaucrat of Europe to the easygoing American official. One of their ideals was efficient and honest government, and no one has made a greater contribution to the realization of this ideal than a Forty-Eighter. It was through the untiring efforts of Carl Schurz that the civil service reform was finally realized.

Another major issue, on which the Forty-Eighters —and most Germans—took an intransigent and unequivocal stand, was slavery. There, too, the Forty-Eighters manifested their logic and their combativeness. They found slavery entirely incompatible with democracy; they demanded its abolition at once. . . .

FURTHER INQUIRY

1. What does the author mean when he says that it was the "political attitude" of the Forty-Eighters rather than the date of arrival by which they can be classified?
2. Is it possible for an immigrant, German, Jew, Irish or Italian, to have dual loyalties—to the country where he was born and to the one where he lives and earns his living?

More than any other immigrant group, the Irish were lured to the cities of America. Here they hoped to find the affluence that had eluded them in Ireland, and a place in American society among the great politicians, artists, and merchants. It took the Irish a long time to achieve this level of success. Why?

6

Urban Irish

by BOB CONSIDINE

THE Irishman setting foot in New York for the first time in the early 1800's found himself in a bustling port which looked like a country town. Behind the tough and dirty waterfront sat the factories and shops, and behind them, houses of dark, weather-beaten wood or bright red brick. Not too far away, the city opened into fields and meadows.

From *It's the Irish,* by Bob Considine (New York: Doubleday & Company, 1961), pp. 66–80. Reprinted by permission of the author.

In the 1800's the immigrant in the city lived amongst a confusion of languages and cultures that were not yet assimilated into the American culture. (Los Angeles County Museum of Natural History)

Sheep grazed on what is now Central Park. He could hear the baas of lambs being led to the slaughter-houses, the clopping of horses' hoofs on the cobblestones, the creaking of carriages and the rumbling of heavy wagons. The raucous voices of sailors mingled with the shouts of street vendors and the cries and laughter of children.

All this was so bewildering to the new immigrant that he was eager to accept the first words of advice and encouragement offered. Much of the time, this was unfortunate because the words came from the New York version of the Liverpool "runner"— the "shoulder-hitter." He sported a green hat, a well-maintained brogue, and a line stretching all the way back to Cork, Limerick, Galway, or wherever

he said he was from. He was quick to help with
the bundles or the babies and steer the trusting immigrant to a "friendly Irish boardinghouse." Usually, these were dilapidated three-story buildings near
the waterfront, with a grog shop* on the ground
floor. The man was invited in for a sip to celebrate
the arrival, and the family led to its cramped room
upstairs. No mention was made of rent for the first
day or two and by the time the family got around
to asking timidly what the charges were, the bill
for the room and the one or more celebrations at
the grog shop often was more money than they had
brought with them to America. The "friendly" Irish
hotelkeeper generously offered to extend credit while
the head of the family found work, but often the
bills piled up faster than the wages, and the Irishman once again found himself at the mercy of a
landlord every bit as unscrupulous as the one from
whom he had escaped.

If the immigrant planned to stay in New York
only a few days before heading into the back country
for a job, he needed travel information and tickets,
and the "shoulder-hitter," or a cohort working as a
passenger agent, practiced additional trickery. The
unschooled Irishman might be sold worthless cou-
pons with pictures of trains or boats on them and
told they were good for travel to Philadelphia or a
ride up the Hudson to Albany. Or the victim might
be put aboard a steamer for Albany with additional
tickets enabling him to continue his journey from
there by rail. Many times, he found he had been
overcharged on train fare, or had underpaid and
must make up the difference, or, worse yet, that no
such train ran to the place he wanted to go.

---

grog shop—bar.

Groups were formed to counter these gyp artists. . . . One of the most effective was the Irish Emigrant Society created in 1841 with the help of Bishop
John Joseph Hughes, later the first Archbishop of
New York. Public officials paid little attention to
these groups at first because they considered it the
duty of the Catholic clergy to watch over and shep-
herd the new arrivals from Ireland, and the Church
did try. But the flood of immigrants was too
great. . . .

Finally, in 1847 the state decided to take an
active interest in the newcomers. With the famine
driving thousands more Irish across the sea, the
New York legislature set up the Board of Commissioners of Emigration, which had among its ten
members the presidents of the Irish and German immigrant societies. The board levied a tax of $1.50
on each passenger to arrive for the support of a
quarantine hospital, an immigration staff, and a
travel and employment aid center. The hard-working
commissioners drove many dishonest runners and
travel agents out of business, but the landing place
of the immigrants had to be changed occasionally
to keep the agents as far away as possible. The
commissioners complained: "The work never ceases,
new schemes of fraud spring up whenever the occa-
sion offers."

The health of immigrants also presented officials
with a major headache. The Irish were so run-down
by inadequate food even before the big famine that
they were the easy targets of disease, and the horrid
holds of the "coffin ships" were excellent breeding
places for the germs. In 1847, emergency hospitals
had to be set up on Staten Island and Long Island
to care for the hundreds of sick. Several towns along
the Hudson River, including Albany, refused to

allow immigrants to leave the steamers, even for an hour, on their way to jobs in the West. In 1849, a severe cholera epidemic, a rugged winter, and a business recession forced the New York commissioners to spend more than $380,000 on the health and relief of immigrants. . . . In 1851, and again in the winter of 1854, epidemics raged in New York, and little wonder when we realize that less than one-third of the city was equipped with a sewer system.

When the Irish moved out of the temporary hotels and boardinghouses, they moved into tenements or old warehouses, or trudged further out to become squatters in a shanty town. . . .

Houses that once sheltered a single family in middle-class comfort became the depressing quarters of a dozen families with six or seven persons crowded into each room. Cellars and attics held not one family but two or three more, separated by thin partitions which often did not even reach the ceiling. Every word, every move could be heard throughout the floor, and the most precious or dreariest moments of family life were public knowledge. All tenants would use the same kitchen, or try to cook in their part of the room, but in either case the result would be the same—a devastating mixture of odors which lasted throughout the day and night and hung on for weeks. Ventilation was poor because most houses had precious few windows at the front and rear, with none in the basements or attics, and windows were kept closed through the long winters for fear that fuel might be wasted. Ten or twenty families might depend upon one or two standpipes for their entire water supply, and many times the pipes were clogged and the water unfit to drink or hardly to wash in. Privies were not far away—not far enough from the water supply—and they contributed to the disease rate by clogging up, overflowing, and seeping into the cellars where people were trying to live.

.   .   .

Lawbreakers multiplied like germs in that primitive environment, and there were nights when police could not cope with all the brawls and petty thefts. The next day, the newspapers would be filled with the names of Irish charged with disturbing the peace, or worse.

But every immigrant group that arrived in this country ragged and rejected, having to fight its way up, has clashed with authority and offended "law-abiding citizens." Once members of the group have been able to break out of their social trap and join the mainstream of American life, most of them become as decent and law-abiding as other citizens. The Irish . . . had an innate respect for the law, and in time it gave them a special place in New York and other cities.

.   .   .

The Irish journalist and orator, Thomas D'Arcy McGee, wanted to get the citified Irish out of their cellars and attics and their children out of the dirty streets of the slums. . . .

The colonization schemes of McGee and others collapsed under some important and determined opposition. Bishop Hughes of New York said most Irishmen would not know how to chop down a tree to clear their land, and would find the hardships and hazards too great to fight. He said he was opposed to all separate Irish settlements, and influential newspapers such as the *Irish News* and the *Freemen's Journal* supported his point of view. As late as 1881, the *Journal*'s editor wrote: "If the Irishmen in New

(UPI)

York are agricultural-minded they have plenty of unoccupied land in Long Island."

Plans for Irish farming communities were proposed in 1904 and again as recently as 1917, but by that time, most of the O'Learys, Finnegans, and

O'Malleys were very much at home in the cities and the towns and not really interested in what remained of the frontier out west.

They loved people, wanted to be near their neighbors, their schools, and their Church. They had put aside their shovels and were through digging ditches and canals.

The Quinns, O'Connors, and O'Callahans had found the jobs they needed to help them crawl out of the hellholes of Five Points and Half-Moon Alley.

FURTHER INQUIRY

1. Why did Irishmen long in this country take advantage of Irishmen new to this country?
2. Why do new immigrants often offend "law-abiding citizens"?
3. How do the experiences of the Irish immigrants compare with those of the German Forty-Eighters? How do you account for the differences? (See Reading #5).
4. To what extent would you say an Irish immigrant farmer was better or worse off than one who remained in the city?

In this tale of an Italian immigrant may
be found some of the factors that made
him leave his homeland and settle in
America. This tale has been repeated
millions of times with an equal number
of variations. Leonardo hoped that in
America his children could "run the race
without the curse of defeat at the start."

7

Leonardo

by ANGELO M. PELLEGRINI

So it was for the sake of his children, yet unborn
and unbegot, that he decided to leave his
parents and San Marco* and to follow his brothers
to America. It was a difficult decision because he

San Marco—a city in Italy.

From *Americans By Choice,* by Angelo M. Pellegrini (New
York: The Macmillan Company, 1956), pp. 194–99. Copyright
© 1956 by Angelo M. Pellegrini. Reprinted by permission of
The Macmillan Company.

knew he would be leaving his parents forever—unless he had been completely wrong in his expectations. He would not leave, as so many did, with the intention of returning for a fresh start in San Marco with American dollars: his would be a permanent break to establish a home in the New World where his children might run the race without the curse of defeat at the start. He loved his parents and he felt they needed the consoling presence of their last son. He might have wavered in his decision had it not been for a letter from America. "I give you my daughter with my blessings," Recchia had written. "I urge you to consider coming to America before it is too late. I myself have no intention of returning to Italy. In a year or two I hope to be able to send for the rest of my family. There is plenty of work here and the pay is good. Life is hard, especially for us who have no education and do not know the language. But it is possible to get ahead. You remember Mateo Crotone who left San Marco in 1898? His eldest son is now a student at the state university. . . ."

. . .

Even for a young man of twenty-four who has never been more than thirty miles away from the village of his birth (he had served his military term in Foggia, a short distance from his home), the distance between San Marco and Chicago was the least impressive fact in his new experience. He saw the corn and the hogs and the cattle, the plains, the rivers and lakes. He felt the spring in the soil of the Mississippi basin. "In America there is land and water," he wrote to Giovannina. "That is all we need." Good soil; good seed. The rest would be inevitable.

But he was not to be a farmer—beyond gardening with fierce zeal his own little plot of earth. And in exactly ten years he was to be so nearly vanquished by land and water that the entire West was to resound with his curses.

Powerful and erect, with a magnificent head of black hair whose color only was to yield to age, he reported for work with his brothers and his father-in-law. His arms and legs were sinewy and supple; his claw-like hands had already acquired the slightly conical curve they were to preserve even in death; his back was tempered. On the hilly, rocky terrain around San Marco he had developed a spread, lumbering stride, a surefooted gait he was never to lose. He was perfectly conditioned to work with pick and shovel and barrow and trowel constructing the streets of Chicago. The necessary skill he acquired easily and quickly. All else he brought to the job: strength, endurance, will.

Pick and shovel and barrow were familiar tools to him. The work of preparing a street or roadbed for the concrete slab did not differ essentially from the work of preparing a field for spring planting. It was all a matter of the movement and distribution of soil. The engineers did the planning and the thinking. In his capable hands the pick and the shovel did the rest. At the end of the day there were food and rest and relaxation and another entry in the savings account.

Cement work, however, was another matter. No weight is so heavy and exhausting as dead weight; and of all dead weights, that sodden mixture of two parts sand, three parts gravel, and one part cement known as concrete mix is the deadest. Merely to look at it is fatiguing; to walk in it with heavy rubber boots is exhausting. A wheelbarrow loaded with

Italians occupy the ranks of most construction companies from ditchdiggers, bricklayers, and concrete-mixers to foremen. And many have started their own companies. (Joe Molnar)

it, especially a barrow with an iron wheel, becomes for an ordinary mortal an immovable object. A shovel filled with concrete seems pinned to the earth with chains. The wet mixture resists the trowel and the float. Neglected but for an instant, it cakes and hardens before it has been bludgeoned into position.

But there is a way of managing the apparently recalcitrant stuff; and Leonardo had the wit to learn the manual dexterity to implement what he learned. For eighteen months, from July, 1907, with an occasional week of idleness because of bad weather, he worked constructing the streets of Chicago. Ten hours a day, six days a week, and frequently on Sundays, Leonardo worked with zest. He was the darling of the bosses who were driven by the superintendents who were driven by the construction tycoons who were driven by a mad passion to complete one job and take on another and to make money and to conquer—what? Leonardo was driven only by an irrepressible exuberance. He mixed and hauled and poured and spread and finished with float and trowel. The sodden mass was putty in his bare hands. He moved it around, tamped it, turned it, stroked it. At his touch, it seemed to lose its weight and immobility. He knew how to manage it and he was esteemed for his skill.

In January, 1909, all construction work ceased because of severe weather. The men were told that there would be little to do for two or three months. Other employment was not easy to find. Leonardo had saved more than enough to send for his wife. What should he do? Should he go fetch her himself? He wanted to see his parents for a last time, perhaps to help them consolidate their small holdings and put their house in order. He wanted also a final look at San Marco in the perspective of his American experience. He consulted his brothers and his father-in-law. It was decided that he should go back and return later with his wife and Recchia's family. And, of course, he would arrive in San Marco just about in time to celebrate his first son's birthday.

. . .

The return to San Marco strengthened his conviction that his decision to leave had been wise. He had no great illusions about America, although he had yet no idea of the extreme of endurance to which his adopted country would drive him and his young bride. For eighteen months he had worked hard in Chicago, perhaps harder than he had ever worked before. But he had returned with dollars in his pocket and good clothes on his back. Regularly, month after month, without haggling, he had been handed his substantial pay envelope. And he had had the novel experience of a sense of achievement. He had seen Italians in Chicago, with no more education than he had, launched into business and advancing in the construction trades; and while he had no particular ambition himself he was inspired by what he observed. He had seen troops of youngsters, varying in age from six to eighteen, well fed and well clothed, with their lunch baskets and books, flocking merrily to school. That sight, more than anything else, had fired his imagination.

By contrast, San Marco seemed even more dismal than it was. He saw there, as he could not have seen without the American experience, not so much the chronic poverty as the utter and complete hopelessness of existence.

. . .

. . . Leonardo, Giovannina, and two sons left San Marco for Seattle, Washington. It was to be their permanent home. Shortly after he had left

The Feast of San Gennaro is an open-market festival that occupies several streets of "Little Italy" and invites the public to come and share in some real Italian food and festivities. (Joe Molnar)

Chicago, his brothers and father-in-law, Mr. Recchia, out of work for the winter, had found employment in the city that had become the "gateway to Alaska" and was to become one of the principal seaports of the Orient trade.

Seattle was, indeed, on the way to becoming a metropolis. Ten years after the discovery of the Alaska gold fields, it had tripled in population: from 80,000 in 1900 to 240,000 in 1910. The young city was booming. Strong backs were needed in the lumbering and construction trades. Millions of cubic yards of dirt were being sluiced into the tide flats from Denny, Dearborn, and Jackson hills to facilitate traffic and to build up the Elliott Bay shore line. Sewer and water mains had to be laid. The city's main arteries had to be constructed athwart the steep slopes and parallel to the waterfront. In a city that was growing rapidly and that was to continue to grow at the rate of 100,000 every ten years for the next forty years, there was much work to do for men like the Patricellis and the Recchias.

They were men who wanted work and who rejoiced in it. Leonardo had no idea of the kind of country to which he was taking his family beyond what Mr. Recchia had told him in a letter. "They say that it is a seaport on the Pacific Ocean," he had written, "close to a country called Alaska, and about two thousand miles west of Chicago. There are Indians there and huge forests. We are told there will be steady work for at least fifty years." Leonardo cared little where Seattle was or how large or who inhabited it. The promise of steady employment was enough to make it attractive. He would manage the rest.

Thus, toward the end of 1910, Leonardo, father of two sons, began his career as pick-and-shovel man in the city of Seattle. In due time he would advance to digging ditches.

FURTHER INQUIRY

1. Why did Leonardo soon feel ready to send for his family?
2. Why did he have a sense of achievement?
3. If Leonardo had been a newcomer of the mid- instead of early 20th century, what difficulties might he have had? What advantages, if any, did he have?
4. Why did San Marco seem even worse than Leonardo remembered it?

This selection, written in 1912 by a Russian immigrant, describes her feelings on the day many years before when her father took her to school in Boston for the first time. Why did the author regard this as the most important day of her life?

8

The Promised Land

by MARY ANTIN

FATHER himself conducted us to school. He would not have delegated that mission to the President of the United States. He had awaited the day with impatience equal to mine, and the visions he saw as he hurried us over the sun-flecked pavements tran-

From *The Promised Land*, by Mary Antin (Boston: Houghton Mifflin Company, 1958), pp. 202–12. Copyright 1940 by Mary Antin. Reprinted by permission of Houghton Mifflin Company.

scended all my dreams. Almost his first act on landing on American soil, three years before, had been
his application for naturalization. He had taken the
remaining steps in the process with eager prompt-
ness, and at the earliest moment allowed by the law,
he became a citizen of the United States. . . .

If education, culture, the higher life were shining
things to be worshipped from afar, he had still a
means left whereby he could draw one step nearer
to them. He could send his children to school, to
learn all those things that he knew by fame to be
desirable. The common school, at least, perhaps,
high school; for one or two, perhaps even college!
His children should be students, should fill his house
with books and intellectual company; and thus he
would walk by proxy in the Elysian Fields of liberal
learning. As for the children themselves, he knew no
surer way to their advancement and happiness.

So it was with a heart full of longing and hope
that my father led us to school on that first day.
He took long strides in his eagerness, the rest of us
running and hopping to keep up.

At last the four of us stood around the teacher's
desk; and my father, in his impossible English, gave
us over in her charge, with some broken word of
his hopes for us that his swelling heart could no
longer contain. I venture to say that Miss Nixon was
struck by something uncommon in the group we
made, something outside of Semitic* features and
the abashed manner of the alien. . . .

All three children carried themselves rather better
than the common run of "green"* pupils that were

Semitic—facial features common to Middle Eastern
    people. Here referring to Jewish features.

green—foreign.

brought to Miss Nixon. But the figure that challenged attention to the group was the tall, straight father, with his earnest face and fine forehead, nervous hands eloquent in gesture, and a voice full of feeling. . . . I think Miss Nixon guessed what my father's best English could not convey. I think she divined that by the simple act of delivering our school certificates to her he took possession of America.

It is not worthwhile to refer to voluminous school statistics to see how many "green" pupils entered school last September, not knowing the days of the week in English, who next February will be declaiming patriotic verses in honor of George Washington and Abraham Lincoln, with a foreign accent, indeed, but with plenty of enthusiasm. It is enough to know that this hundred-fold miracle is common to the schools in every part of the United States where

The accumulation of knowledge, whether it be Talmudic study . . . or a public school education, has always been a strong and cohesive force in Jewish culture.

(Arthur Tress)

immigrants are received. And if I was one of Chelsea's hundred in 1894, it was only to be expected, since I was one of the older of the "green" children, and had had a start in my irregular schooling in Russia, and was carried along by a tremendous desire to learn, and had my family to cheer me on.

I was not a bit too large for my little chair and desk in the baby class, but my mind, of course, was too mature by six or seven years for the work. So as soon as I could understand what the teacher said in class, I was advanced to the second grade. This was within a week after Miss Nixon took me in hand. . . .

There were about half a dozen of us beginners in English, in age from six to fifteen. Miss Nixon made a special class of us, and aided us so skillfully and earnestly in our endeavors to "see-a-cat," and "hear-a-dog-bark," and "look-at-the-hen," that we turned over page after page of the ravishing history, eager to find out how the common world looked, smelled and tasted in the strange speech. The teacher knew just when to let us help each other out with a word in our own tongue—it happened that we were all Jews—and so, working all together, we actually covered more ground in a lesson than the native classes, composed entirely of the native tots.

But we stuck—stuck fast—at the definite article;* and sometimes the lesson resolved itself into a species of lingual gymnastics, in which we all looked as if we meant to bite our tongues off. Miss Nixon was pretty, and she must have looked well with her white teeth showing in the act; but at the time I was too solemnly occupied to admire her looks. I did take great pleasure in her smile of approval, whenever I pronounced well; and her patience and per-

---

definite article—"the."

severance in struggling with us over that thick little
word are becoming to her even now, after fifteen
years. It is not her fault if any of us to-day give a
buzzing sound to the dreadful English TH.

.   .   .

Whenever the teachers did anything special to help
me over my private difficulties, my gratitude went
out to them, silently. It meant so much to me that
they halted the lesson to give me a lift, that I needs
must love them for it. Dear Miss Carrol, of the
second grade, would be amazed to hear what small
things I remember, all because I was so impressed
at the time with her readiness and sweetness in taking notice of my difficulties.

Says Miss Carrol, looking straight at me:

"If Johnnie has three marbles and Charlie has
twice as many, how many marbles has Charlie?"

I raise my hand for permission to speak.

"Teacher, I don't know vhat is tvice."

Teacher beckons me to her, and whispers to me
the meaning of the strange word, and I am able to
write the sum correctly. It's all in the day's work
with her; with me, it is a special act of kindness
and efficiency.

She whom I found in the next grade became so
dear a friend that I can hardly name her with the
rest, though I mention none of them lightly. Her
approval was always dear to me, first because she
was "Teacher," and afterwards, as long as she lived
because she was my Miss Dillingham. Great was my
grief, therefore, when, shortly after my admission to
her class, I incurred discipline, the first, and next
to last, time in my school career.

The class was repeating in chorus the Lord's
Prayer, heads bowed on desks. I was doing my best
to keep up by the sound; my mind could not go

beyond the word "hallowed," for which I had not
found the meaning. In the middle of the prayer a
Jewish boy across the aisle trod on my foot to get
my attention. "You must not say that," he ad-
monished in a solemn whisper; "it's Christian." I
whispered back that it wasn't, and went back to the
"Amen." I did not know but that he was right, but
the name of Christ was not in the prayer and I was
bound to do everything that the class did. If I had
any Jewish scruples, they were lagging away behind
my interest in school affairs. How American this
was: two pupils side by side in the schoolroom,
each holding to his own opinion, but both submit-
ting to the common law; for the boy at least bowed
his head as the teacher ordered.

But all Miss Dillingham knew of it was that two
of her pupils whispered during the morning prayer,
and she must discipline them. So I was degraded
from the honor row to the lowest row, and it was
many a day before I forgave that young missionary;
it was not enough for my vengeance that he suffered punishment with me. Teacher, of course,
heard us both defend ourselves, but there was a
time and a place for religious arguments, and she
meant to help us remember that point.

I remember to this day what a struggle we had
over the word "water," Miss Dillingham and I. It
seemed as if I could not give the sound of W; I
said "vater" every time. Patiently my teacher worked
with me, to get my stubborn lips to produce that W;
and when at last I could say "village" and "water"
in rapid alternation, without misplacing the two
initials, that memorable word was sweet on my
lips. For we had conquered, and Teacher was
pleased. . . .

If I was eager and diligent, my teachers did not

sleep. As fast as my knowledge of English allowed, they advanced me from grade to grade, without reference to the usual schedule of promotions. My father was right, when he often said, in discussing my prospects, that ability would be promptly recognized in the public schools. Rapid as my progress was, on account of the advantages with which I started, some of the other "green" pupils were not far behind me; within a grade or two, by the end of the year. . . .

FURTHER INQUIRY

1. Why did high school and college seem such remote goals to the author's father?
2. Why did he have high hopes his children would get there?
3. Was it fair to force Jewish children to recite the Lord's Prayer, a non-Jewish prayer? Would this be required today?

The most famous Chinatown in America
is home to thousands of Chinese and
an attraction to thousands of tourists.
To what extent is Chinatown a ghetto?

9

Chinatown, West

by CALVIN LEE

A FTER the San Francisco fire of 1906, Will Ir-
win, one of the first writers to appreciate the
beauty of the old Chinatown, wrote:

From *Chinatown, U.S.A.*, by Calvin Lee (New York: Double-
day & Company, Inc., 1965), pp. 89–101. Copyright © 1965 by
Calvin Lee. Reprinted by permission of Doubleday & Company,
Inc., and Nannine Joseph.

The market places of San Francisco's Old Chinatown mirrored the poverty and filth of life in Hong Kong. (The Bettmann Archive)

It is gone—gone with the sea-gray city which encircled it. The worse order changeth, giving place to the better; but there is always so much in the worse order which our hearts would have kept! In a newer and stronger San Francisco rises a newer, cleaner, more beautiful Chinatown. Better for the city, oh, yes! and better for the Chinese, who must come to modern ways of life and health if they are to survive among us. But . . . where is the dim reach of Ross Alley, that horror to the nose, that perfume to the eye? Where are those broken dingy streets in which the Chinese made an art of rubbish?

If one can ever be thankful for a disaster, here indeed is such a situation. If it were not for the fire of 1906 San Francisco might never have had the most charming Chinatown in the country. Not the artificial contrived type built in Los Angeles but a place where Chinese live, work, and play, a place which has a "lived-in" feel; adding to its culture and beauty, San Francisco's Chinatown feels the pulse of the metropolis. But, being on the Western shores and the largest port for newcomers to the New World from the Orient, it is always replenished with new immigrants and thus never completely loses the charm of the way of the old country.

The north end of San Francisco's Chinatown, at Grand and Broadway, is where the Chinese live and shop. As early as 1854 the area from Washington Street to Sacramento along the east side of DuPont (now called Grant) and the alleys of this vicinity were spoken of as "little China." Here the first Chinese merchants established their stores and teahouses. By 1877 it was six blocks in length running north and south on DuPont Street from California to Broadway, and two blocks wide from east to west on Sacramento, Clay, Commercial, Washington, Jackson, Pacific, and Broadway Streets, from Kearney to Stockton, crossing DuPont.

On every side red and gilt greeted the eye. Large wooden signs with carved Chinese characters hung outside the places of business. Every nook and corner along the sidewalks was crowded by the stalls

of curbstone merchants selling vegetables, fruits and
sweetmeats, and by specialists offering their services—cobblers, razor sharpeners, and tinkers, each
occupying not more than two or three feet. Some
of these paid a small rental, but many were free
tenants. In some parts of Chinatown were cellars
where the poorest and least fortunate Chinese lived.

For gifts such as lacquered boxes, vases, and
ivory carvings one used to go to Chine Lee's on
Kearney Street or King Tai's under the Palace Hotel
or Lung's on Sacramento Street, between Mont-
gomery and Kearney.

A "joss house" called the "Eastern Glorious
Temple" was owned and run by Dr. Lai Bo Tai, a
Chinese herb doctor. By the late 1870's there were
two principal Chinese theaters, both on Jackson
Street between Kearney and DuPont, where traditional Chinese plays depicting historical events were
put on. Some old frame buildings were still standing by the 1870's. By and large the buildings were
of plain American architecture but the theaters, the
restaurants, the joss houses, and some other buildings were fancifully decorated and lit up with Chinese lanterns of all sizes and shapes that fluttered
and flickered in front of all public places.

On Jackson Street was a silversmith, and men
making finger rings, hairpins, and other Chinese
ornaments. The Chinese nearly monopolized the
manufacturing of overalls in California at one time
and the work was done right on DuPont. Also to
be found on this street were shirtmakers, a shoe
factory, and a tin shop. Everywhere was a smell
which was characteristic of Chinatown in the late
1800's. As described by Reverend O. Gibson it
was ". . . the smell of cigars, and tobacco leaves wet
and dry, dried fish and vegetables; all these toned

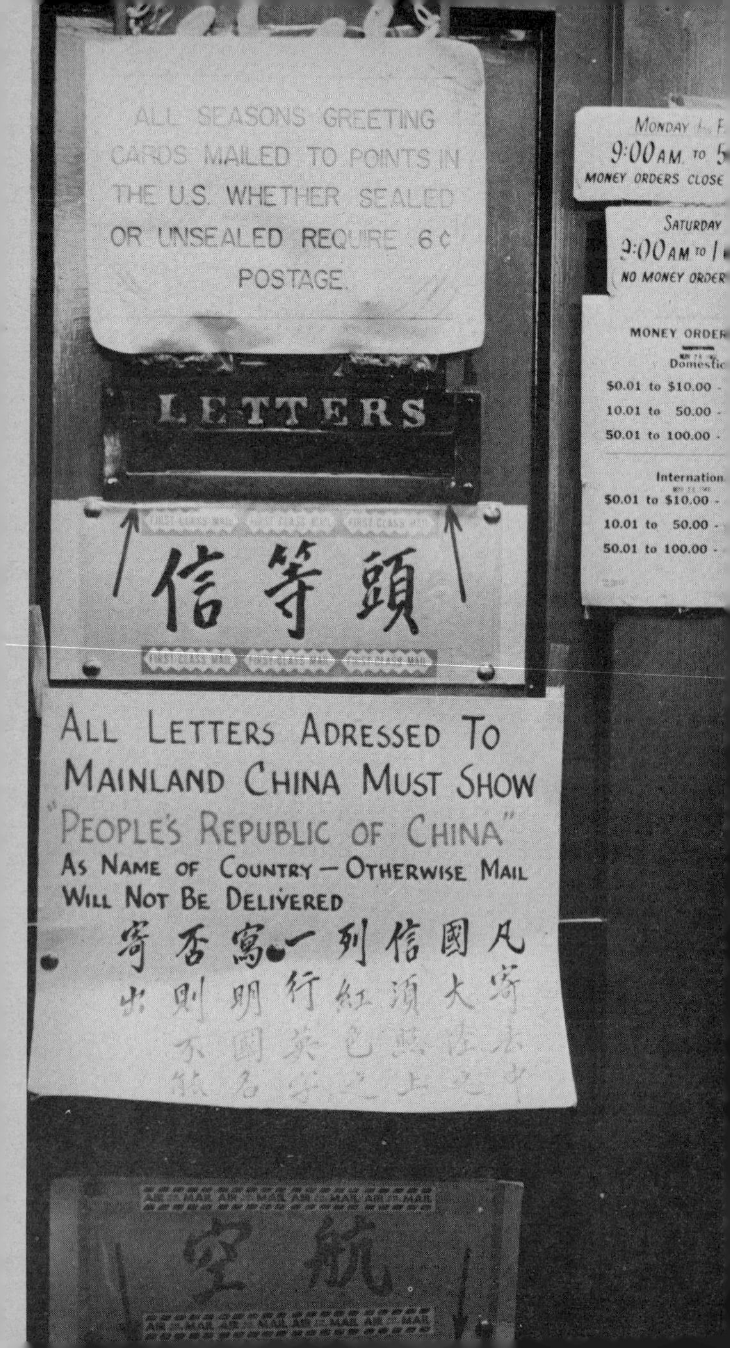

ALL SEASONS GREETING
CARDS MAILED TO POINTS IN
THE U.S. WHETHER SEALED
OR UNSEALED REQUIRE 6¢
POSTAGE.

LETTERS

信 等 頭

ALL LETTERS ADRESSED TO
MAINLAND CHINA MUST SHOW
"PEOPLE'S REPUBLIC OF CHINA"
AS NAME OF COUNTRY — OTHERWISE MAIL
WILL NOT BE DELIVERED

凡寄往中
國須大陸之
信照紅色之上
一行寫明英字之
否則國名
寄出不能

空 航

MONDAY ⸬ F
9:00 AM TO 5
MONEY ORDERS CLOSE

SATURDAY
9:00 AM TO 1
NO MONEY ORDER

MONEY ORDER
Domestic
$0.01 to $10.00 -
10.01 to 50.00 -
50.01 to 100.00 -

Internation
$0.01 to $10.00 -
10.01 to 50.00 -
50.01 to 100.00 -

Chinatown is not immune to change. . . . (Arthur Tress)

to a certain degree by what may be called a shippy smell, produced a sensation upon the olfactory nerves* of the average American."

This area from California Street to Broadway, the birthplace of Chinatown, is now the "little China" within Chinatown. Look carefully and you will still find some of the old pioneer firms. There is Wo Kee at Grant Avenue, established in 1856 as a supplier of food and clothing to the early Chinese miners. A store specializing in Chinese slippers at 857 Grant, has survived over a hundred years. Quong Lee, a general mercantile store was established in 1865 as a men's clothing shop. At the corner of Washington Street and Wentworth Place since 1880 is Tuck Hing, the first poultry and meat market in Chinatown. Tai Hing Lung, importer–exporter, is still being managed by the family who founded it in 1885.

All over the north end of Grant Avenue the storekeepers each morning lay out their fresh meats, fish, and vegetables for eager Chinese housewives who come to buy their provisions for the day. Freshly roasted ducks, squabs, chickens, suckling pigs are hung in the store windows. For the busy housewife some stores even have prepared vegetables and other vegetables ready to be eaten. Among these shoppers are some old women with their hair tied back in a bun, wearing black Chinese dresses and walking in a way which indicates that their feet were bound in childhood.*

Watch the salesmen, each equipped with a long

olfactory nerves—those found in the nose.

It was an ancient custom to bind the feet of Chinese girls, in the interests of beauty, to prevent them from growing.

blue apron, giving individual attention to their customers. Watch them add up the bill on an abacus*
seemingly as quickly as an IBM machine might do
it.

Chinatown is not immune to change imposed by
the modern age. Interspersed throughout this colorful district are some elaborate stainless steel and glass
storefronts and self-service supermarkets dealing
with Chinese goods. Though Chinese herbs and spices
are lined up on the shelves, at the end of the line is
not an abacus but an automatic cash register, in
shiny contrast to the warm dark wooden storefronts
of the tiny grocery stores with bamboo baskets filled
with Chinese vegetables. The large carved wooden
signs with gilded Chinese characters are being replaced by neon lights and aluminum even at this
end of "little China."

The casual observer may not know that these
stores have taken the place of the large industries
which once occupied this end of town. Gone are
the cigar factories, the shoe factories, and the furniture factories. Gone are the merchants' stalls
above which hung narrow boxes to which, with the
help of a stepladder, the storekeeper climbed and
slept in. Can one really regret their departure? Not
only has the appearance of Chinatown changed,
new business and new professions have been added.
The four-story signs of the large and flourishing
savings and loan associations prominently light up
the whole north end of Grant Avenue. Here is the
secret of the Chinese. Their thriftiness and wise investment in real estate has tided them over good
and bad times. Also found in this area in the new
office buildings are insurance brokers, travel agen-

---

abacus—a wire rack with beads used for calculating.

cies, real estate companies, medical, dental, legal
and accounting services, many of them run by
second and third generation Chinese-Americans.
These changes have taken place only since World
War II.

In this neighborhood also are hardware stores
where one can purchase a *wok,* a large round pan
for cooking, and a *choy doh,* the famous Chinese
cleaver. Clothing stores, some of them with un-
likely Chinese names such as Winky's Children's
Shop and Kaye's Footwear Store, are indications
of the changing order.

FURTHER INQUIRY

1. Why does the author say San Francisco's
   Chinatown should be thankful for a disaster?
2. What does the author mean when he says,
   "Chinatown feels the pulse of the metropolis?"
3. How did Chinatown help the Chinese immigrant? Did it hurt the Chinese immigrant
   as well?

An American-born Japanese (Nisei), whose real name is Kazuko Monica Itoi, tells of her childhood experiences in a Japanese waterfront community in Seattle.

10

Nisei Daughter

by MONICA SONE

FATHER had often told us stories about his early life. He had come from a small village in the prefecture of Tochigi-ken. A third son among five brothers and one sister, Father had gone to Tokyo to study law, and he practiced law for a few years before he succumbed to the fever which sent many

From *Nisei Daughter*, by Monica Sone (Boston: Little, Brown & Company, 1953), pp. 5–15. Copyright 1953 by Monica Sone. Reprinted by permission of Atlantic-Little, Brown and Company, and Brandt & Brandt.

young men streaming across the Pacific to a fabulous
new country rich with promise and opportunities.

In 1904 Father sailed for the United States, an
ambitious young man of twenty-five, determined to
continue his law studies at Ann Arbor, Michigan.
Landing in Seattle, he plunged into sundry odd jobs
with the hope of saving enough money to finance
his studies. Father worked with the railroad gang,
laying ties on virgin soil; he toiled stubbornly in
the heat of the potato fields of Yakima; he cooked
his way back and forth between Alaska and Seattle
on ships of all sizes and shapes; but fortune eluded
him. Then one day he bought a small cleaning and
pressing shop on Tenth and Jackson Street, a wagon
and a gentle white dobbin, "Charlie." The years
flew by fast, but his savings did not reflect his
frenzied labor. With each passing year, his dream
of Ann Arbor grew dimmer.

At last Father's thoughts turned toward marriage.
About this time the Reverend Yohachi Nagashima
—our grandfather—brought his family to America.
Grandfather Nagashima was a minister of a Con-
gregational church in Sanomachi, about twenty miles
north of Tokyo in Tochigi-ken prefecture. He had
visited the United States twice before on preaching
missions among the Japanese. Grandfather had been
impressed with the freedom and educational opportunities in America. He arrived in Seattle with his
wife, Yuki, three daughters, Yasuko, my mother
Benko, and Kikue, twenty-two, seventeen, and sixteen years of age respectively, and two round-eyed
sons, Shinichi and Yoshio, six and four years.

Mother and her sisters sailed into the port looking like exotic tropical butterflies. Mother told us
she wore her best blue silk crepe kimono, Yasuko
chose a deep royal purple robe, and Kikue, a soft

rose one. Their kimonos had extravagantly long, graceful sleeves, with bright red silk linings. Over their kimonos, the girls donned long, plum-colored, pleated skirts, called the *Hakama,* to cover the kimono skirts that flipped open as they walked. Shod in spanking white *tabis*—Japanese stockings—and scarlet cork-soled slippers, the young women stood in tense excitement at the rails of the ship. . . .

Father heard of the Nagashimas' arrival. He immediately called to pay his respects. Seeing three marriageable daughters, Father kept going back. Eventually he sent a mutual friend to act as go-between to ask for the hand of the first daughter, Yasuko, but the friend reported that Mr. Nagashima had already arranged for Yasuko's marriage to a Mr. Tani. Undaunted, Father sent his friend back to ask for the second daughter, Benko. Mother said that when her father called her into his study and told her that a Mr. Itoi wanted to marry her, she was so shocked she fled to her room, dived under her bed and cried in protest, "I can't, Otoh-san, I can't. I don't even know him!"

Her father had got down on his hands and knees and peered at her under the bed, reprimanding her sternly. "Stop acting like a child, Benko. I advise you to start getting acquainted with Mr. Itoi at once."

And that was that. Finally Mother gave her consent to the marriage, and the wedding ceremony was performed at the Japanese mission branch of the Methodist Episcopal Church at Fourteenth and Washington Street. . . .

In January, 1918, their first child was born, Henry Seiichi—son of truth. Shortly after, Father sold his little shop and bought the Carrollton Hotel on Main Street and Occidental Avenue, just a stone's

throw from the bustling waterfront and the noisy
railroad tracks. It was, in fact, on the very birth
site of Seattle when the town began its boisterous
growth with the arrival of pioneer Henry Yesler
and his sawmill on the waterfront. In its early days,
the area south of Yesler Hill, where we lived, was
called Skid Road because loggers used to grease
the roads at intervals to help the ox teams pull the
logs down to the mills. Nearly a hundred years
later, the district bore the name Skidrow, a cor-
rupted version of Skid Road, with its shoddy stores,
decayed buildings, and shriveled men.

.   .   .

When Father took over the hotel in 1918, the
building fairly burst with war workers and servicemen. They came at all hours of the day, begging to
sleep even in the chairs in the hotel lobby. Extra
cots had to be set up in the hallways.

Father and Mother loved to tell us how they
had practically rejuvenated the battered, flea-ridden
Carrollton by themselves. Father had said firmly,
"If I have to manage a flophouse, it'll be the clean-
est and quietest place around here." With patience
and care, they began to patch the aches and pains
of the old hotel. . . .

All the while Father tried to build up a choice
selection of customers, for even one drunkard on a
binge always meant fist fights and broken furniture.
Father quickly found that among the flotsam* of
seedy, rough-looking characters milling around in
Skidrow were men who still retained their dignity
and self-respect. There were lonely old men whose
families had been broken up by the death of wives
and departing children, who lived a sober existence

---

flotsam—wreckage.

The streets of the slums are playgrounds to many immigrant children. One of the games they play involves chasing a rat out into the street and then beating it to death with sticks and clubs found in nearby garbage pails. (Arthur Tress)

on their meager savings or their monthly pension allotment. Father also took in sea-hardened mariners, shipyard workers, airplane workers, fruit pickers and factory workers. He tried to weed out petty thieves, bootleggers, drug peddlers, perverts, alcoholics and fugitives from the law. . . .

For our family quarters, Mother chose three outside rooms looking south on Main Street, across an old and graying five-story warehouse, and as the family increased, a fourth room was added. . . .

At first glance, there was little about these simple, sparse furnishings to indicate that a Japanese family occupied the rooms. But there were telltale signs like the *zori* or straw slippers placed neatly on the floor underneath the beds. On Mother's bed lay a beauti-

ful red silk comforter patterned with turquoise,
apple-green, yellow and purple Japanese parasols.
And on the table beside the local daily paper were
copies of the *North American Times,* Seattle's Japa-
nese-community paper, its printing resembling rows
of black multiple-legged insects. Then there was the
Oriental abacus board which Father used once a
month to keep his books.

.   .   .

In the kitchen were unmistakable Oriental traces
and odors. A glass tumbler holding six pairs of red
and yellow lacquered chopsticks, and a bottle of
soy sauce stood companionably among the imita-
tion cut glass sugar bowl and the green salt and
pepper shakers at the end of the table. The tall
china cabinet bulged with bright hand-painted rice
bowls, red lacquered soup bowls, and Mother's
precious *somayaki* tea set.

.   .   .

In the pantry, the sack of rice and gallon jug of
shoyu stood lined up next to the ivory-painted
canisters of flour, sugar, tea and coffee. From a
corner near the kitchen window, a peculiar, pungent
odor emanated from a five-gallon crock which
Mother kept filled with cucumbers, *nappa* (Chinese
cabbage), and *daikon* (large Japanese radishes),
immersed in a pickling mixture of *nuka,* consisting
of rice polishings, salt, rice and raisins. The fer-
mented products were sublimely refreshing, deli-
cious, raw vegetables, a perfect side dish to a rice
and tea mixture at the end of a meal.

Among the usual pots and pans stood a dark red
stone mixing bowl inside of which were cut rows
and rows of minute grooves as on a record disc. The
bowl was used to grind poppy seeds and *miso* (soy-
beans) into soft paste for soups and for flavoring

Almost every ethnic group in America has its own newspaper. Many have radio and television programs also. (Fujihira, Monkmeyer)

Japanese dishes. I spent many hours bent over this
bowl, grinding the beans into a smooth, fine paste
with the heavy wooden club. For all the work that
went into making *miso shiru,* a soybean soup, I
thought it tasted like sawdust boiled in sea brine.
Mother told me nothing could be more nutritious,
but I could never take more than a few shuddering
sips of it.

·   ·   ·

So we lived in the old Carrollton. Every day,
amidst the bedlam created by four black-eyed, jet-
propelled children, Father and Mother took care of
the hotel. Every morning they went from room to
room, making the beds and cleaning up. To help
speed up the chores, we ran up and down the
corridors, pounding on doors. We brutally woke the
late sleepers, hammering with our fists and yelling,
"Wake up, you sleepyhead! Wake up, make bed!"
Then someone would think of pushing the linen cart
for Father and the rest of us would rush to do the
same. We usually ended up in a violent tussle. . . .
Sometimes on a wintry evening, we crowded
around the kitchen table to watch Father, bath
towel-apron draped around his waist, whip up a
batch of raisin cookies for us. It wasn't everybody's
father who could turn out thick, melting, golden
cookies. We were especially proud that our father
had once worked as a cook on romantic Alaska-
bound freighters.

·   ·   ·

I thought the whole world consisted or two or
three old hotels on every block. And that its population consisted of families like mine who lived in a
corner of the hotels. And its other inhabitants were
customers—fading, balding, watery-eyed men, rough-
tough bearded men, and good men like Sam, Joe,

Peter and Montana who worked for Father, all of whom lived in these hotels.

It was a very exciting world in which I lived.

FURTHER INQUIRY

1. The author's father dreamed of studying law in America. But his dream did not come true. Why not?
2. According to Japanese custom in those days, marriages were "arranged." Would you like an "arranged" marriage?
3. To what extent would you say the author's family had become "assimilated" Americans?
4. It was Japanese such as these who were forced to move into special camps during World War II. Why were Japanese-Americans forced into special camps and not German-Americans?

The author, a Jew and a Southerner, is
known for his penetrating comments on
American life, manners and society. He
writes here of his memories as a Jewish
immigrant immediately after his arrival
in America. Are memories of one's past
reliable guides to the present?

11

Only in America

by HARRY GOLDEN

MY uncle Koppel (K. Berger) was twenty years
old when he came to America. The day after
his arrival he opened a small butcher shop on
Scammel Street, on New York's Lower East Side.
For the next three years he opened up his shop at

From *Only In America*, by Harry Golden (Cleveland: The
World Publishing Company, 1958), pp. 64–68. Copyright 1944,
1948, 1949, 1951, 1953, 1954, © 1955, 1956, 1957, 1958 by
Harry Golden. Reprinted by permission of The World Publishing
Company.

six o'clock in the morning, cooked his meals on a stove in the back of the store, and pushed the meat block up against the front door to sleep. What English he learned he picked up from the truck drivers, who delivered the meat and the poultry. There was nothing unusual about this. There were thousands of immigrants who lived, worked and died within the confines of a few city blocks. But with Koppel Berger it was to be different, because Uncle Koppel had imagination, courage, ability, and, above all, he seemed to know what America was all about.

It was 1904 and all America was singing, "Meet me in St. Louey, Louey, meet me at the fair . . ." and my immigrant uncle took the lyrics literally. He arrived in St. Louis, Missouri, with five hundred dollars, a wife, and a vocabulary of about thirty words of broken English. He acquired a lease on a rooming house, which accommodated thirty guests. Again he worked night and day. His wife did the laundry, cleaned the rooms, and made the beds; Uncle Koppel carried the baggage, roomed the guests, kept the accounts, carried the coal, made the hot water, and told his guests that he was an employee so that he could also run all their errands. The St. Louis Fair was a success, and so was Koppel Berger. After two years, he and his wife and infant son returned to New York with a little over eight thousand dollars.

Up on Broadway at 38th Street was the old Hotel Normandie, which was not doing so well under the management of the great prizefighter, the original Kid McCoy (Norman Selby).

With a vocabulary of about seventy-five words of broken English, Uncle Koppel took over the lease on this 250-room hotel in the heart of the theatrical district. Of course, even a genius must have some luck, too, and we must concede that Koppel Berger

EVA TANGUAY

Eva Tanguay is credited with changing the tone of vaudeville "from sentiment to sex." Though she was a well-paid
and famous star, the rule of Victorian morality in this
period made her unwelcome in the more exclusive hotels.
(Theater Collection, The New York Public Library at
Lincoln Center. Astor, Lenox, and Tilden Foundations.)

acquired the Hotel Normandie at exactly the right moment. New York and America were becoming "hotel-minded"; in addition, the theatre was entering upon its greatest era, a "golden age" such as we shall never see again. Between 1907 and 1927, there were literally hundreds and hundreds of road shows and stock companies; burlesque was in all its glory; dozens of opera "extravaganzas" were playing all over the country; vaudeville was at its all-time peak; and on Broadway itself, there were at least one hundred and fifty attractions produced each year.

In those days, "actors" and "actresses" were not particularly welcome at the best hotels. In fact, many New Yorkers will remember the signs on some small hotels and rooming houses, "Actors Accommodated."

In various stages of their careers, Uncle Koppel's Hotel Normandie was "home" to such players as Nat Wills, Wilton Lackaye, Cissie Loftus, Grant Mitchell, Lionel and John Barrymore, Otto Kruger, Doc Rockwell, W. C. Fields, Julian Eltinge, Tully Marshall, Tyrone Power, Sr., Dustin Farnum, Marie Cahill,* and, of course, hundreds of lesser-known personalities. They had fun with Koppel Berger. They mimicked his accent; they made jokes of his hotel from the vaudeville stage; and they played tricks on the live fish he had swimming in a bathtub every Friday. Mike Jacobs, too, got started at the Hotel Normandie under Uncle Koppel. The man who later controlled the champion, Joe Louis, as well as the "prize-fight" business itself, started with a small ticket stand at the hotel, and the first time I ever saw Mike, he was sliding down the lobby

---

All entertainers of the past.

banister like a kid, with his brother Jake "catching" him. I used to go to the Normandie once a week after school. My older brother Jack was the night clerk, and my mother insisted that he have a "Jewish" meal every Friday night, so I took the Broadway streetcar to 38th Street, carrying a large carton which included a pot of chicken soup, gefilte fish, horseradish, boiled chicken, and *tsimmiss*.* My mother had arranged with the chef at the old Offer's Restaurant to let me use his stove to get the stuff hot again. It was quite a Friday afternoon, all around.

My brother, who later acquired some hotels of his own, coined the phrase about "sleeping on the sign." A guest came in and was told that the only room available would cost $2.50. The guest said, "You've got $1.50 on the sign," and my brother told him, "Try and sleep on the sign."

Most of the one million dollars Uncle Koppel made in the Hotel Normandie came during World War I, when he put dozens of cots in the lobby and in the upstairs hallways, to take care of the tremendous influx of job-seekers and servicemen. The elevator in the Normandie was the old cable variety, with the operator sitting in a swivel chair and pulling the cable up and down.

One night Uncle Koppel rented the swivel chair to a. guest who had to get a few hours' sleep.

During this fabulous era of profits at the Normandie, Uncle Koppel was acquiring other hotels —the Old Calvert, the Nassau, the Aberdeen, the Riviera in Newark; and, finally, the famous old Martinique Hotel at the intersection of Broadway and Sixth Avenue.

---

tsimmiss—vegetable or fruit pudding.

On the day Koppel Berger took possession of the Martinique, he stopped talking Yiddish. No one will ever know why he stopped talking Yiddish, or how he expected to get along on a vocabulary of about one hundred and fifty words of broken English; but he saw it through to the bitter end. My mother tried to trap him many times into using a Yiddish word, but he never fell for the bait. Not only did he stop talking Yiddish, but he no longer "understood" it.

My mother would say something to him and he'd look at her with big innocent eyes and motion to one of us in a helpless sort of way to act as an "interpreter." She would become exasperated, call to him in Yiddish, and when he turned to one of his "interpreters," she would rattle off a string of *klulas* (Yiddish curse words), each of which was a masterpiece; but old Koppel Berger did not move a muscle or bat an eye. He simply smiled tolerantly, turned to one of us children and asked, "Vot did she set?"

As you would expect, Uncle Koppel liquidated the Hotel Normandie at the very "top." A year before the crash, he sold the hotel to a fellow (a Mr. Lefcourt), who couldn't wait to put up a forty-story building, but who met the terrible Depression before he reached the twenty-fifth floor. In his last years, K. Berger retired to California, but he never stopped making money. At the age of eighty-three, he closed a deal for a large and profitable citrus business on the coast.

With it all, I believe Uncle Koppel was a sentimental man. I remember while I was in high school, he once asked me to do some "writing work" for him. He took me down to the basement of the old Normandie Hotel where there was a mountain of baggage left by guests who had not paid the room rent in past years.

He wanted me to find the last known address of each, for an advertisement, as provided by law, before he could sell the stuff at auction. I looked over the vast numbers of suitcases and trunks, and said, "Uncle Koppel, these actors sure took away a lot of money from you."

Koppel Berger gently patted an old battered trunk with a faded "Orpheum Circuit" imprint, and said, "These actors *gave* me a lot of money."

FURTHER INQUIRY

1. To what extent is it possible for other newcomers to follow the example described here?
2. Could the author's uncle be called an "assimilated" immigrant?
3. Koppel Berger, the author says, "seemed to know what America was all about." What was America all about then? What is it all about today?

The popular gospel singer tells of her
hopes and fears as she moved from her
home in New Orleans to the great city
of Chicago. Would you agree or disagree with Miss Jackson when she says
". . . in Chicago the Negro found the
open door"?

12

Movin' On Up

by MAHALIA JACKSON *with*
EVAN MCLEOD WYLIE

A FTER Fred* was gone, I knew the time had
come for me to go, too. While I'd been growing up some of the colored people had begun drift-
ing away from New Orleans. Many of the young
colored men began to go on from their riverboat

Fred—Miss Jackson's cousin who encouraged her singing.

From *Movin' On Up,* by Mahalia Jackson with Evan McLeod
Wylie (New York: Hawthorn Books, Inc., 1966), pp. 39–48.
Copyright © 1966 by Mahalia Jackson.

jobs to become chefs and waiters and Pullman car porters on the big express trains. They rolled out across the United States and the trains carried them away from New Orleans and the Mississippi forever. Today their grandchildren are living in states from Connecticut to California.

My uncle Porter was one of those who advanced himself this way. He had moved on up to a job as a headwaiter in a first-class boardinghouse in New Orleans, where he managed a dining room that seated sixty people. Then he decided to take to the railroads.

In those days the great trains that ran across the country were in their glory. The steamboats were on their way out, but the railroads were the wonder of the country. They had sleeping cars and fancy dining cars and they streaked out of New Orleans to the north and to the east and to the west.

.   .   .

Young colored men like my uncle Porter took a mighty pride in their food and their service. They wore starched white jackets and they polished the brass floors in those railroad car kitchens with acid until they shone so it was like walking on gold. They leaned out of the windows of those big crack trains and saw the whole United States go by. They learned about the country and they banded together in a great workingmen's union that came to be known as The International Brotherhood of Sleeping Car Porters. A. Philip Randolph, one of the famous leaders of the NAACP, rode the trains on his way to become president of the union.

Today many of the country's Negro doctors and lawyers are the sons of Pullman porters and waiters who raised their families and put them through college by riding the railroad. Now those days have almost passed. The airplanes and buses are stealing more people away from the railroads every year. Now they've started letting colored folks into the dining cars to sit down and eat a meal, but the age of the railroads is almost over and today there's no pride in good service and the food costs so much you can hardly swallow it.

Other colored people had started going up from New Orleans to Chicago. Some of them came back and told us how Negroes lived better up there— how they rode in buses and trolleys with white people and even had their own automobiles.

My uncle Emanuel went up to Chicago. He worked there for a while as a bricklayer and he made enough money to pay for all of us back home, too. . . .

In 1928, when I was just sixteen, I finally went, using money I had saved from being a nursemaid and laundress. My aunt Duke was against it. She said I was going to a sinful place and tried to stop me. But I was almost a young woman, tall and strong as an ox with a will of my own, and I told her I had to go whether she liked it or not.

My aunt Hannah, who was going back to Chicago, took me along with her on Big Number Four—the express train that ran straight through up North. Before we left we cooked up some food and took it along in a big basket. We sat up in our seats for two nights and a day and ate it. It was many years before I ever saw the inside of a railroad dining car or a Pullman berth. I'd been traveling for years all over the North as well as the South, from New York to San Francisco, before I was able to get a berth to sleep in on a train or to eat in the dining car without being put behind a screen so the white folks wouldn't have to see me.

The twenties were good times for the Negro migrating to the North. (UPI)

It was December when we got to Chicago. The wind was blowing snow around and it was so cold my bones were shaking. When we came out of the railroad station I started off walking down the street, but my aunt Hannah hustled me right into a taxi that a white man was driving. Down in New Orleans you'd never go near a white man's taxi, but Aunt Hannah said this was Chicago and the man wouldn't mind driving us. Sure enough, he never said a word about it and seemed glad to have us for his fare.

.   .   .

Aunt Alice had a big, clean apartment and she found room for me in one of the rooms with my young cousins. The neighborhood was not far away

144

from the stockyards. Lots of colored people worked there and out in the Gary steel mills. . . .

The South Side was home to all the Negroes who had come streaming up to Chicago from the Deep South since long before World War I. You didn't meet many colored people from Georgia, the Carolinas and Virginia. Those people mostly went up to New York and Philadelphia and Baltimore and Washington. But you met all the folks who had come up from Louisiana and Mississippi and Arkansas and Kentucky.

.   .   .

The Negroes stayed in Chicago and they built up their life there until it became the greatest business center for the Negro race in America. Whole townloads of colored people came up North to Chicago and brought their own doctors and ministers and undertakers with them. They lived on the South Side in little clusters of communities that kept growing and expanding toward each other until they joined up. They moved into the white neighborhoods that had held the Germans, the Poles, the Irish, the Italians and the Jews and all the other people who had come to Chicago as immigrants and struggled to start a new life there.

The white people fought to keep the colored families out. They tried to stop them with bombs and riots, but Negroes kept right on coming. They rented rooms and they bought houses. Later, when the white people gave up and moved away, the Negroes would buy their businesses and the churches and synagogues that the white congregations couldn't take with them.

When I first saw it, getting off the train from New Orleans, the South Side was a Negro city. It had Negro policemen and firemen and schoolteach-

The ghetto is home, the place where the black man runs the show. (Arthur Tress)

ers. There were Negro doctors and lawyers and aldermen. Here and there you'd still run across a Polish or Italian neighborhood mixed in with the colored, but mostly you could go for miles and miles without seeing a white person. The South Side, like Harlem, was the place the Negro went home to after working to earn his money in other parts of the city. When he got there he could lay down his burden of being a colored person in the white man's world and lead his own life.

The country was still enjoying the fat years of the 1920's, and in Chicago the colored world was in full bloom. Never before had Negroes lived so well or had so much money to spend. I'll never forget what a joy it was to see them driving up and down Southern Parkway and Michigan Boulevard in big, shiny touring cars and strolling in the evening, laughing and talking and calling out happily to each other. The men wore cream-colored spats and derbies and carried walking sticks. Their women had fur coats and led little dogs on leashes. Many of the houses on Michigan Avenue were mansions and the people that lived there had diamonds and silks and drove Rolls-Royces. They could easily afford them because some Negroes had become millionaires in the real estate and insurance businesses.

The church was the core of the Negro social life in those days, even more so than it is now, and thousands of us went to church two or three times a day on Sunday and just as often during the week. You had to get in line an hour ahead of time at the big churches if you wanted to be seated for the Sunday service, and the people arriving in big limousines would make your eyes pop.

While I lived with my aunts, and all along Prairie and Indiana Avenues, Negroes were buying houses

and fixing them up really nice. They were planting
flowers and shrubs and putting up awnings on their
balconies and terraces, and talking about the good
times and spending their money.

Chicago still had all the jazz musicians that had
come up from New Orleans and Memphis and St.
Louis; they hadn't moved on yet to New York
City. There were black and tan music halls and
cabarets. White people used to come out in crowds
to the South Side to hear Louis Armstrong and
Earl "Father" Hines at the Grand Terrace Ball-
room. At the Royal Gardens and Grande Theater
there was vaudeville every night with star per-
formers like Ethel Waters and the Mills Brothers
and the Whitman Sisters. I stood in line to hear
Bessie Smith at the Avenue Theater and sat in my
seat so thrilled to hear her as she filled the whole
place with her voice that I never went home until
after they put us out and closed up for the night.

.   .   .

In our apartment, my little cousin Nathaniel slept
on a couch in the dining room. Little Alice, who
was only nine years old, slept in with her mother.
Aunt Hannah had a couch in the living room and I
had a couch on the sunporch. In that way, my aunts
could cut the rent a bit by letting out one of the
bedrooms to a boarder, and we always had a railroad dining car waiter living in one of those bedrooms when he wasn't away on train trips to New
York.

Every morning except Sunday I'd be up before
six o'clock so I could ride with my aunt Alice on
the elevated train to the North Side. I can still remember the darkness and cold of those days. The
winter wind in Chicago just takes your breath away
and, while I was saving up to buy a warm coat, all

I had to cut that wind was sweatshirts and sweaters. Shivering in that elevated train, watching the snow blow and swirl in the streetlights and the sun just starting to come up—those were the days when I was low and lonely and afraid in Chicago. The cold and the noise seemed to beat on me and the big buildings made me feel as if I'd come to live in a penitentiary. Oftentimes, I wished I could run away back home to New Orleans.

But after I got up to Chicago, I stuck. I didn't go back to New Orleans for fifteen years. And whatever I am today I owe to Chicago, because in Chicago the Negro found the open door.

FURTHER INQUIRY

1. "There's no pride in good service," says Miss Jackson. Why does she feel that pride in good service has been lost? Do you agree that it has been lost?
2. Compared with other Negro migrants who came from the South, do you think Mahalia Jackson was better or worse off?

In this selection the author describes the forces that encouraged Puerto Rican migration to the mainland and the kind of life Puerto Ricans found when they got here. "The young people are throwing over some of the things their parents believed in," says the author of this story of Puerto Rican youth. What things are probably being overthrown?

13

Coming of Age in Nueva York

by PETE HAMILL

THE Puerto Ricans came to New York to live better. It was as simple as that. It was a trickle at first, in the 1920s and 1930s, because the ticket on the Bull Line cost more than a man could earn in a year, and the trip was long and dangerous and the city was a mean, hard place then, if your skin

From "Coming of Age In Nueva York," by Pete Hamill, *New York* Magazine, Vol. 2, November 24, 1969, pp. 33–47. Copyright © 1969 by New York Magazine Company. Reprinted by permission of International Famous Agency, Inc.

was dark and your language was Spanish. Some of
the earliest worked on the Brooklyn piers, unloading
bananas, with the spiders large enough to play baseball with and the old Bull Line captains keeping the
men in line. A few drifted into the South Bronx
and the Lower East Side, to the places that were
being abandoned by the Jews and the Irish who
were starting to make it. But most went to East
Harlem, El Barrio, where 110th and Lex was the
center of the world, and you could buy *plátanos* at
the Park Avenue market and rice and beans from
people you knew.

They came here because the island they left behind was the sinkhole of the Caribbean, with a life
expectancy of 32, a place where the American rulers
would sit around the palace in white duck while
jíbaros died in the mountains from yaws and para-
sites. . . . New York might have been a strange and
alien place to those early arrivals, but it was better
than dying young.

And then the migration started to build. Puerto
Ricans were different from others who had come to
New York from the slums of Europe. Most impor-
tantly, they were citizens and had been so by act of
Congress since 1917. So they were not immigrants,
they were migrants. They fought in the First World
War and all the wars after, and if there were large
numbers of Puerto Ricans then who wanted independence from the United States, it was only
because the United States had treated them so shab-
bily. . . .

And through all those years, before the explo-
sions of the years after the Second World War, the
dream remained the same: to come to New York,
make money, learn a trade, and go home to Puerto
Rico. . . .

The forces of magic and the supernatural are strong among
many Puerto Rican migrants. There are small salons where
a visitor can have his future predicted by a palm-reader,
and shops selling a curious mixture of voodoo dolls and
Christian statues. (Nathan Farb)

Every day the planes unloaded, and the people
were pathetic to look at. Their suitcases were card-
board, tied with rope, holding everything they possessed. They did not understand the cold; they had
seen snow only in the movies; they arrived in January in sports shirts, with vague addresses scribbled
in pencil on the backs of envelopes, and hardly any
money. . . .

There was no place to go except to the slums, of
course: to the dark spiky landscapes of fire escapes
and mean streets and doors covered with metal.
There was never enough heat, and they plugged

towels into the cracked windows to keep out winter, and bought a hundred thousand miles of felt tape to tack around doors, and made blankets from left-over clothes, and carried drums of kerosene up to the stoves in the parlor, and kept the gas ovens going at night. It was never warm enough. . . .

But the Puerto Ricans have done what all the immigrants did. They have endured. . . .

They've purchased through grief and work and endurance that special thing which the sociologists work so hard at dehumanizing: mobility.

That mobility has freed the first brigades of the emerging Puerto Rican middle class in this town (with the same set of conflicts over loyalties to those left behind which afflicts the black middle class). But there are still hundreds of thousands living in desperate situations, and the Puerto Ricans are in fact still at the bottom of the city's economic ladder. . . .

Some of this can be attributed to the problem of education. An analysis by the Puerto Rican Forum shows that of those Puerto Ricans who finish high school, 90 per cent have been getting a general diploma, 8 per cent a vocational degree, and only 1.2 per cent the academic diploma leading to college. In the elementary schools, there is still an insistence on teaching kids in English, which they sometimes do not know, with the result that or-dinarily bright kids are stunned and humiliated before they have much of a chance to learn anything at all.

Another factor is that the Puerto Ricans are the youngest people in the city, with a median age (ac-cording to a 1966 City University study) of 19.1, compared to 38.6 for whites and 26.1 for nonwhites.

This indicates a group in flux, and the educational statistics at present might be quite misleading; there might be an explosion of academic diplomas any year now. . . .

There are still many Puerto Ricans working for unconscionably low salaries in sweatshops and factories run by gangster unions; a union like the International Ladies Garment Workers Union still does not have real representation of Puerto Ricans at its highest level despite the overwhelming number of Puerto Ricans in its rank and file. Narcotics remains a poison, with some communities, like Hunts Point in the Bronx, practically devastated by the problem. Heroin addicts were practically unknown in Puerto Rico itself until those who were contaminated started coming home from New York. The Puerto Rican street gangs, which were so prominent in the 1950s (the Enchanters, the Dragons, the Latin Gents, etc.), have largely disappeared, not because of especially enlightened social workers, but because a junkie doesn't have much time for gangbusting. ("It's not cool anymore to be in the hitter's bag, man," one kid told me last year.)

.　　　.　　　.

The younger generation of Puerto Ricans are also making the whole thing move in another way. They don't feel sorry for themselves, they have been here all their lives, they have a sense of what must be done and how to go after it. Some are starting militant Puerto Rican organizations, like Barrio Nuevo in East Harlem. Others are going the college route. . . . Increasingly, the younger generation is political, and if that has set up a generation gap of sorts, it is only because the Puerto Ricans are finally part of something larger. . . .

The younger people seem more interested in specifics. I remember going to a meeting in East Harlem the day after the 1967 riots took place. Ted Velez and Andrew Segarra and Torres and a lot of others had worked long into the night trying to cool the riots, and this meeting, in a school auditorium, was held to try to make sure that that trouble would not flare up again. There were representatives from the city and from the police to listen to the grievances of the young people who had done most of the fighting and bottle-throwing. Their initial grievance, as it had been in other circumstances in other sections of the city, was with the Tactical Patrol Force. The TPF, these kids felt, was an armed guard of cops from outside the district, cops who could not possibly know who was who in East Harlem, who probably did not know much about Puerto Ricans, and who had reacted brutally and without sensitivity to the first outbreak of trouble. That was predictable. But when that had been cleared out of the way, they got down to the real issues. One kid got up, his voice laden with emotion, and said very loudly: "All right, to hell with that for a minute. I want to know *why* in the goddam hell you can't get the garbage off 112th Street? Just get the garbage and we'll believe you." . . .

Politically, the Puerto Ricans are certainly on the move. The near victory of Herman Badillo in the Democratic primary has probably removed "the Puerto Rican thing" the way John F. Kennedy's 1960 victory changed the myth about Catholics running for President. . . .

What seems to be forming is a special breed: the New York Puerto Rican. One who listens to La Lupe and the Beatles, who reads the *Times* and *El*

The Puerto Ricans have endured the hardships of migration and now add a new life and spirit to the city of New York. (Arthur Tress)

Diario, who can move around the East Side pubs
and still make it up to the Broadway Casino. He is
a baseball fan, because of Orlando Cepeda and
Roberto Clemente and a dozen other stars who
came up from the island; but he probably does not
look for the score of the Ponce–Caguas game anymore; he more than likely roots for the Mets (I
have yet to meet a Puerto Rican who cared for pro
football or rooted for the Yankees). But he no
longer needs to go to prizefights to identify vicari-
ously with heroes. He seems to be breaking down
between two New York cultural traditions, with a
touch of the third: the Puerto Rican with the can
of beer in a paper bag playing dominoes on the
street is the Irish Puerto Rican; the guy selling the
beer in the *bodega* is the Jewish Puerto Rican;
the guy starting to move into numbers and narcotics
in East Harlem is the Mafia Puerto Rican. Ah, give
me your tired, your poor. . . .

FURTHER INQUIRY

1. Drug addiction, which was not a problem
   among Puerto Ricans living on the island,
   has become a devastating problem among
   Puerto Ricans living in New York. What
   reasons may account for this? What can be
   done about it?
2. The younger generation of Puerto Ricans
   is described as more political than the older
   generation. Why is this so?
3. How do you account for the relatively slow
   progress among Puerto Ricans in learning to
   speak English?
4. Among the demands Puerto Rican activists
   have made were (1) clean the garbage more

frequently, (2) provide a place to play dominoes, and (3) dancing once in a while. To what extent are these reasonable or unreasonable demands?

This selection is from the book "La Raza" which itself is a Spanish word meaning the race. The race in this instance refers to the Mexican-Americans and to Mexican immigrants who are originally descended from the ancient and magnificent Aztec, Toltec and Mayan cultures which made the Southwest take on much of the character it now has. The selection below describes the plight and the exploitation of the illegal Mexican immigrant ("wetback") whose labor is used on the farms of California.

14

The Man with the Guitar

by STAN STEINER

IT is four o'clock in the morning on the Mexican border. The lights of the Border Station flicker on the deserted streets. A truck parks in a dark alleyway. The driver lights a cigarette, and waits. Hundreds of people with small bundles move noiselessly past the yawning border guards. The driver spits contemptuously at the ragged ones. These are his human cargo.

From *La Raza: The Mexican-Americans*, by Stan Steiner (New York: Harper & Row, 1969), pp. 133–37, 139. Copyright © 1969, 1970 by Stan Steiner. Reprinted by permission of Harper & Row, Publishers, Inc., and Bartold Fles Literary Agency.

The Old Guitarist, by Pablo Picasso. (Courtesy of the Art Institute of Chicago)

One by one the men and women crawl under the loose tarpaulin on the back of the truck. No one talks. When the truck is full the driver stomps out his cigarette and roars northward. He drives one hundred, two hundred, three hundred, four hundred miles without stopping, except for gas. The local city ordinances along the way are not gracious to truckloads of Mexicans. He knows the police will not stop him if he does not stop.

Inside the truck there may be thirty or forty men and women. The stagnant air is nauseating. Even the breeze under the tarpaulin of sweetly sick desert dawn does not help. An old man may urinate in tension; his fear pollutes the crowded, stifling truck.

"Are you sick?" someone says.

"Yes," the old man says.

They nod. What is there to say when there is nothing they can do?

Going to the fields, in every truck I have been in, there is a man who can sing. He may have a harmonica or he may have a guitar. It doesn't matter. If he sings at that lonely hour he sings to himself.

> When I left Hermosillo
> My tears fell like rain,
> But the little red flower
> Consoled my pain.
>
> I am like a coyote
> Who eats poppies, and goes
> Trotting off sideways—
> Where? Nobody knows.

. . .

The open, rumbling trucks of the *coyotes* and the old buses, abandoned by the regular companies, are not all that bad. Like the village buses of ancient

vintage in old Mexico they wheeze through the
deserts of the Southwest. Every year one or two of
these fail to make it across the railroad crossing,
somewhere on a country road, and the *campesinos**
are flung out, like chickens, to die beside the high-
way.

One ordinary morning in the little town of Calexi-
co, in the Imperial Valley of California, there are
twenty-three trucks and old buses waiting for their
human cargoes. In one hour, from 4:00 to 5:00
A.M., Dr. Samuel Yellen, a city councilman from
nearby Brawley, using a hand counter, clocked those
who crossed the border at that single customs station. He counted 1,404 campesinos, in that dim,
predawn hour.

"These are poor people," says Dr. Yellen. "In
Mexico the farm workers earn fifteen cents an hour,
those who are lucky enough to get jobs. The
corporations—Litton Industries, Fairchild Camera,
Hughes Aircraft—who have factories south of the
border pay their workers as little as two dollars a
day. So naturally these poor people think that working for fifty cents an hour in the United States is
paradise. It's worth the suffering, they think."

And so they come, singing of sorrows and nos-
talgia. The exodus goes on. It is the same in every
border town, on every morning, from Brownsville
to Tijuana.

"The most deprived classes of Chicanos are constantly replenished by new immigrants, both permanent and temporary, from Mexico," says Hector
Abeyta, the director of California's Manpower Opportunities Project of the U.S. Department of Labor.
"Almost all of the immigrants are from the poorest

---

campesinos—farm workers.

people in that country, who come north in search of opportunity.

"Mexican Americans have a higher proportion of foreign born than any other ethnic group in the United States," Abeyta says.

It is whispered in the barrios that tens of thousands of people are neither citizens nor legal residents of the United States. "They jump!" says Eduardo Pérez, a community leader of East Los Angeles. "They disappear. They vanish into the barrios. They live like anyone. They don't hide in the Disneyland of the U.S.A.," says Pérez. "They are bold."

The old *corrido* says:

> Who puts water in his wine
> Makes it thin and weak;
> Who never has known life
> Of living may not speak.

And yet the emigrant is fearful. . . .

"La Cucaracha" was the hymn of the Mexican Revolution, but the man with the guitar sings it differently. He *is* a cockroach. He is invisible. Not only the memory of his illegality, but the ever-present reality of deportation.

It is officially guessed that as many as 40,000 Mexican citizens come to Los Angeles alone yearly. (The population of San Antonio is estimated to increase by 50,000 every year.) One barrio leader of East Los Angeles says that he unofficially guesses the annual influx in that city may be 100,000. He is asked, Why, if this is so, is the population of the barrios not many millions? "The border is a two-way street," he says. "Maybe 100,000 come; maybe 100,000 go."

Once he has crossed over, he is in jeopardy. He may be "cowed and thankful" for his family's safe arrival. "After all, isn't he, the Mexican immigrant, a guest, an *ensimado,* and an *arrimado,* a parasite?" writes Antonio Gómez in *Con Safos:* "Is it not unthinkable for a guest to complain about the lodging and odd jobs that his host has given him? What voice does a guest have in operating the host's household?"

The migrant is ridiculed by the Chicanos. The young Los Angeleans sometimes refer to the newcomer contemptuously as a "TJ." Literally the nickname means that he comes from Tijuana. Where he crosses the border does not really matter so much as his awkward manner, unfashionable dress, and servility. He is cowed by the affluence of the city and overwhelmed by the speed of the freeways. The poorest of the poor, the TJ has no choices. He must accept the lowest jobs, live in the worst barrios, suffer the insults of both Chicano and Anglo. He has only his family to help him. Life is precarious and work is scarce.

An emigrant to the barrios has to know how to laugh at his dilemma.

> I went to the border
> To see who knew me:
> And at eleven that night
> The police arrested me.

> They arrested me
> In the American style:
> As if I was a criminal
> With pistol in hand.

Cesar Chavez, leader of the striking National Farm Workers Union, is helping to change the song of the migrants. The NFWU is the first effective union in the history of this country's migratory farm workers. (Wide World)

He is jailed for "being a fighting cock," the emigrant of the *corrido* laments. In his cell he is offered "a recipe of the House of Congress," the warrant for his arrest. "Do you know why you're in prison?" asks the judge. He doesn't. The emigrant replies seriously, putting on a formal manner, "I don't expect a temple or crystal palace." But the judge is not amused; he sentences the emigrant to jail, and to himself the emigrant thinks, I have been arrested "because of my stupidity." He laughs at himself.

> I come from Morelia
> Dreaming of the dollars,
> Bought shoes and a hat,
> Even put on trousers.

Hundreds and thousands of *vaciladas, corridos,* ballads, serenades, *posadas, aires de la tierra,* and popular tunes tell of the journey of the migrants and of living in the barrios. In the life of an "unlettered people," words are music and history is sung. "Wherever you go, you shall go singing," Huitzilopochtli, the war and sun god of the Aztecs, had commanded. It is still so. The odyssey of the migrants into the urban cities is rewritten by every man with a guitar. "Out of poverty, poetry; out of suffering, song," is the old Mexican proverb. Songs are the true history of the migrations of La Raza.

> Now I am confused.
> I am a shoemaker.
> But here I am a camel,
> With a pick and shovel.

What good is my trade
If machines are faster;
When I make two shoes,
They make one million.

They told me the money
Lay in the streets
Like girls and theatres—
A utopia of sweets.

.   .   .

Like the troubadour of old he goes down the road
not quite knowing where he is going. He knows only
he has nowhere else to go. He goes singing.

FURTHER INQUIRY

1. Why does the man with the guitar sing sad
   songs? What do they tell of the hopes and
   fears of the illegal Mexican-immigrant?
2. Why is crossing the border illegal?
3. Why does the truck driver know that the
   police won't stop him? Where is the truck
   heading?
4. Why are the illegal immigrants willing to
   work for fifty cents an hour?
5. Should such illegal immigration from Mexico
   be stopped altogether?

In this selection the late American President describes the contributions of the anonymous immigrant to American life. An anonymous immigrant is one without fame but whose hard work contributed to America's success. In seeking their own freedom and fortune they "helped strengthen the fabric of liberty in American life." So writes the former President. How did anonymous immigrants help strengthen America?

15

The Immigrant Contribution

by JOHN F. KENNEDY

OSCAR Handlin* has said, "Once I thought to write a history of the immigrants in America. Then I discovered that the immigrants *were* American history." In the same sense, we cannot really

---

Oscar Handlin—eminent historian, specializing in the immigrant.

From *A Nation of Immigrants*, by John F. Kennedy (New York: Harper & Row, 1964), pp. 64–68. Copyright © 1964 by Anti-Defamation League of B'nai B'rith and Hamish Hamilton, London. Reprinted by permission of Harper & Row, Publishers.

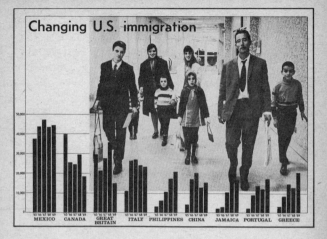

Changing U.S. immigration

50,000
40,000
30,000
20,000
10,000
0

'65 '66 '67 '68 '69   '65 '66 '67 '68 '69   '65 '66 '67 '68 '69   '65 '66 '67 '68 '69   '65 '66 '67 '68 '69   '65 '66 '67 '68 '69   '65 '66 '67 '68 '69   '65 '66 '67 '68 '69   '65 '66 '67 '68 '69
MEXICO   CANADA   GREAT BRITAIN   ITALY   PHILIPPINES   CHINA   JAMAICA   PORTUGAL   GREECE

(Peter W. Main, Photo Staff, *The Christian Science Monitor*)

speak of a particular "immigrant contribution" to
America because all Americans have been immigrants or the descendants of immigrants; even the
Indians migrated to the American continent. We can
only speak of people whose roots in America are older
or newer. Yet each wave of immigration left its own
imprint on American society; each made its distinctive "contribution" to the building of the nation and
the evolution of American life. Indeed, if, as some of
the older immigrants like to do, we were to restrict
the definition of immigrants to the 42 million people who came to the United States *after* the Declaration of Independence, we would have to conclude
that our history and our society would have been
vastly different if they all had stayed at home.

As we have seen, people migrated to the United
States for a variety of reasons. But nearly all shared
two great hopes: the hope for personal freedom and
the hope for economic opportunity. In consequence,
the impact of immigration has been broadly to con-

firm the impulses in American life demanding more
political liberty and more economic growth.

.   .   .

A German farmer wrote home from Missouri in
1834,

> If you wish to see our whole family living
> in . . . a country where freedom of speech obtains,
> where no spies are eavesdropping, where no sim-
> pletons criticize your every word and seek to detect
> therein a venom that might endanger the life of the
> state, the church and the home, in short, if you wish
> to be really happy and independent, then come here.

Every ethnic minority, in seeking its own freedom,
helped strengthen the fabric of liberty in American
life.

Similarly, every aspect of the American economy
has profited from the contributions of immigrants.
We all know, of course, about the spectacular immigrant successes: the men who came from foreign
lands, sought their fortunes in the United States and
made striking contributions, industrial and scientific,
not only to their chosen country but to the entire
world. . . .

But the anonymous immigrant played his indispensable role too. Between 1880 and 1920 America
became the industrial and agricultural giant of the
world as well as the world's leading creditor nation.
This could not have been done without the hard
labor, the technical skills and the entrepreneurial
ability of the 23.5 million people who came to
America in this period.

Significant as the immigrant role was in politics
and in the economy, the immigrant contribution to
the professions and the arts was perhaps even great-

er. Charles O. Paullin's analysis of the *Dictionary of American Biography* shows that, of the eighteenth- and nineteenth-century figures, 20 percent of the businessmen, 20 percent of the scholars and scientists, 23 percent of the painters, 24 percent of the engineers, 28 percent of the architects, 29 percent of the clergymen, 46 percent of the musicians and 61 percent of the actors were of foreign birth—a remarkable measure of the impact of immigration on American culture. And not only have many American writers and artists themselves been immigrants or the children of immigrants, but immigration has provided American literature with one of its major themes.

Perhaps the most pervasive influence of immigration is to be found in the innumerable details of life and the customs and habits brought by millions of people who never became famous. This impact was felt from the bottom up, and these contributions to American institutions may be the ones which most intimately affect the lives of all Americans.

In the area of religion, all the major American faiths were brought to this country from abroad. The multiplicity of sects established the American tradition of religious pluralism and assured to all the freedom of worship and separation of church and state pledged in the Bill of Rights.

So, too, in the very way we speak, immigration has altered American life. In greatly enriching the American vocabulary, it has been a major force in establishing "the American language," which, as H. L. Mencken demonstrated thirty years ago, had diverged materially from the mother tongue as spoken in Britain. . . .

Immigration plainly was not always a happy experience. It was hard on the newcomers, and hard as well on the communities to which they came. When poor, ill-educated and frightened people disembarked in a strange land, they often fell prey to native racketeers, unscrupulous businessmen and cynical politicians. Boss Tweed* said, characteristically, in defense of his own depredations in New York in the 1870's, "This population is too hopelessly split into races and factions to govern it under universal suffrage, except by bribery of patronage, or corruption."

But the very problems of adjustment and assimilation presented a challenge to the American idea—a challenge which subjected that idea to stern testing and eventually brought out the best qualities in American society. Thus the public school became a powerful means of preparing the newcomers for American life. The ideal of the "melting pot" symbolized the process of blending many strains into a single nationality, and we have come to realize in modern times that the "melting pot" need not mean the end of particular ethnic identities or traditions. Only in the case of the Negro has the melting pot failed to bring a minority into the full stream of American life. Today we are belatedly, but resolutely, engaged in ending this condition of national exclusion and shame and abolishing forever the concept of second-class citizenship in the United States.

Sociologists call the process of the melting pot "social mobility." One of America's characteristics has always been the lack of a rigid class structure. It has traditionally been possible for people to move up the social and economic scale. Even if one did not succeed in moving up oneself, there was always

---

Boss Tweed—an unscrupulous political boss, and leader of Tammany Hall.

the hope that one's children would. Immigration is by definition a gesture of faith in social mobility. It is the expression in action of a positive belief in the possibility of a better life. It has thus contributed greatly to developing the spirit of personal betterment in American society and to strengthening the national confidence in change and the future. Such confidence, when widely shared, sets the national tone. The opportunities that America offered made the dream real, at least for a good many; but the dream itself was in large part the product of millions of plain people beginning a new life in the conviction that life could indeed be better, and each new wave of immigration rekindled the dream.

This is the spirit which so impressed Alexis de Tocqueville, and which he called the spirit of equality. Equality in America has never meant literal equality of condition or capacity; there will always be inequalities in character and ability in any society. Equality has meant rather that, in the words of the Declaration of Independence, "all men are created equal . . . [and] are endowed by their Creator with certain unalienable rights"; it has meant that in a democratic society there should be no inequalities in opportunities or in freedoms. The American philosophy of equality has released the energy of the people, built the economy, subdued the continent, shaped and reshaped the structure of government, and animated the American attitude toward the world outside.

The *continuous* immigration of the nineteenth and early twentieth centuries was thus central to the whole American faith. It gave every old American a standard by which to judge how far he had come and every new American a realization of how far he might go. It reminded every American, old and

new, that change is the essence of life, and that
American society is a process, not a conclusion. The
abundant resources of this land provided the founda-
tion for a great nation. But only people could make
the opportunity a reality. Immigration provided the
human resources. More than that, it infused the
nation with a commitment to far horizons and new
frontiers, and thereby kept the pioneer spirit of
American life, the spirit of equality and of hope,
always alive and strong. "We are the heirs of all
time," wrote Herman Melville, "and with all nations
we divide our inheritance."

FURTHER INQUIRY

1. In this selection the author says that the
   "melting pot" concept is in effect the process
   of social mobility. What does he mean? Do
   you agree?
2. Traditionally, the author continues, it has
   been possible for Americans to move up in
   the social and economic scale because America lacked a rigid class structure. To what
   extent would you agree or disagree with this
   view?
3. To what extent has the concept of second-
   class citizenship been eliminated? Where
   does it exist? How can it be eliminated?
4. The author Herman Melville wrote, "We
   are the heirs of all time and with all nations
   we divide our inheritance." What did he
   mean?

Urban Faces —
A Photographic Essay

by SHALMON BERNSTEIN

Who lives in the city?

Who commutes?

Who visits?

Who is born in the city?

And who grows up here, gleaning what he can from the intermingling of social classes, nationalities, races, and age groups, before moving on?

Who participates in city life on a twenty-four hour basis for a lifetime?

And who ends his city life at 5 p.m. each evening, escaping to the suburbs?

All these people are a part of the city at some time. The city is the melting pot of ideas and opinions as well as nationalities and races.

Notes

Suggestions for Additional Reading

Index

Notes

THE PROBLEM AND THE CHALLENGE

1. Based on Richard F. Shepard, "The West Side: A Polyglot of Races, Creeds and Cultures," *The New York Times,* October 25, 1968, pp. 49, 50, 92.

2. George F. Mowry, *The Urban Nation* (New York: Hill and Wang, 1965), pp. 1–5.

3. John F. Kennedy, *A Nation of Immigrants* (New York: Harper and Row, 1964), p. 5.

4. Mark Tannenbaum, "American Negro Myths and Realities," *American Jewish Committee,* January-February, 1954, p. 3.

5. Maldwyn Allen Jones, *American Immigration* (Chicago: University of Chicago Press, 1960), p. 213.

6. Nathan Glazer and Daniel Patrick Moynihan, *Beyond the Melting Pot* (Cambridge, Mass.: The MIT Press, 1963), p. 97.

7. Christopher Rand, *The Puerto Ricans* (New York: Oxford University Press, 1958), p. 52.

8. For a more complete treatment of this theme, see *The Negro in the City* in this series.

9. Mahalia Jackson with Evan McLeod Wylie, *Movin' On Up* (New York: Hawthorn Books, Inc., 1966), p. 47.

10. Based on *Report of the National Advisory Commission on Civil Disorders* (New York: Bantam Books, 1968), pp. 240–43.

11. *Ibid.,* p. 390.

12. Jackson, *op. cit.,* p. 51.

13. Oscar Handlin, *The Newcomers* (Cambridge, Mass.: Harvard University Press, 1959), pp. 7–8.

14. Quoted in Kennedy, *op. cit.,* p. 58.

15. Handlin, *op. cit.,* pp. 59–60.

16. *Ibid.,* p. 104.

17. Glazer and Moynihan, *op. cit.,* pp. 128–29.

18. Handlin, *op. cit.,* p. 118.

19. Glazer and Moynihan, *op. cit.,* p. 17.

20. *Ibid.,* p. 20.

Suggestions for Additional Reading

1. Glazer, Nathan, and Daniel Patrick Moynihan, *Beyond the Melting Pot.* Cambridge, Mass.: The MIT Press, 1963.

2. Handlin, Oscar, *The Newcomers.* Cambridge, Mass.: Harvard University Press, 1959.

3. Handlin, Oscar, *Race and Nationality in American Life.* New York: Little, Brown and Company, 1957.

4. Jones, Maldwyn A., *American Immigration.* Chicago: University of Chicago Press, 1967.

5. Leinwand, Gerald, *The Negro in the City.* New York: Washington Square Press, 1969.

6. Senior, Clarence, *The Puerto Ricans.* Chicago: Quadrangle Books, 1965.

7. Treverso, Edward, *Immigration: A Study in American Values.* Boston: D. C. Heath, 1964.

Index